D1380517

wise , vetars

Book No **0203673**

30109 002036732

A
HISTORY OF
LANCASHIRE

A HISTORY OF LANCASHIRE

P.J. Gooderson

RESERVE STOCK

B. T. Batsford Ltd *London*

To my Mother and Father

RESERVE STOCK

BEXLEY LIBRARY SERVICE
ACC. No. 01244 Bk HS
1 - DEC 1980 £5.95
Cl No. 942.76 Goo

First published 1980
© P J Gooderson 1980

ISBN 0 7134 2588 1

Typeset by Tek-art Ltd, London SE20
Printed in Great Britain by
Redwood Burn Ltd
Trowbridge and Esher
for the publishers
B T Batsford Ltd
4 Fitzhardinge Street
London W1H 0AH

CONTENTS

ACKNOWLEDGMENT

Lancashire is a county enormously rich in archive material and secondary works, at least for the period covering the last three hundred years. Space has precluded the use and acknowledgment of more than a few of these here. A whole lost world invites discovery, and only a fleeting glimpse of it can be provided in these few pages. Anyone interested in the regional history of the north-west has only to do as I have done and to ask the help of archivists and librarians. All whom I have encountered have been most patient and long-suffering, and I would recommend to fellow students, especially, the staffs of Bacup, Blackburn, Bolton, Burnley, Bury, Kirkby, Lancaster, Liverpool, Lostock Hall, Manchester, Oldham, Preston, Rochdale, Salford, Warrington and Wigan Public Libraries, the Lancashire Record Office and the University Libraries of Lancaster and Manchester. I am most grateful to Mr T. Kelsall of Quernmore for his permission to make use of the Cragg and Kelsall diaries, and to the City of Manchester Cultural Services for permission to use the Bury MSS. Further information has been supplied by the museums of Lancaster, Liverpool and the University of Manchester and by the Walker Art Gallery, Liverpool. I have received invaluable specialist help from Mr W.D. Amos, Mr G. Greenough, Mrs A. Helm, Mr M.J. Hopkinson, Dr J.D. Marshall, Mr C. Mellor, Mr D. O'Connor, Dr A.J.N.W. Prag, Dr D.C. Shotter, Mr D. Swarbrick, and from my former colleagues, Messrs T.C.F. Darley and R. Poole. Mrs B. Baker of Batsford has guided this book through its final stages of publication. Finally, I owe a special debt to members of my family, without whose support this book would not have been published.

The Author and Publishers would like to thank the following for their permission to reproduce the illustrations used in this book: Bolton Central Reference Library, 14; Blackpool Library, 24; The British Library, 9; Doreen Brotherton, 6; Burnley Public Library, 22; Camera Press Ltd, 30; Department of the Environment (Crown Copyright reserved), 10; Department of Leisure Services, Bury, 25; J. Hardman, 27; Lancashire Life, 7, 26; Lancaster City Museum, 16; Liverpool Public Libraries, 23; Liverpool Record Office, 13; Manchester Public Libraries, 8, 15, 18, 19, 21, 29; The Manchester Museum, 1, 2; J.D. Marshall, Map 2; C. Mellor, coats of arms, p. 45; E.J. Morten Ltd, 20; Ordnance Survey/Robert Hale, Map 1; Trevor L. Southworth, 12; D. Swarbrick, 3; Walker Art Gallery, Liverpool, 17. Nos. 4 and 5 are reproduced by Courtesy of the Trustees of the British Museum. Nos. 11 and 28 are from the Publishers' collection.

LIST OF
ILLUSTRATIONS

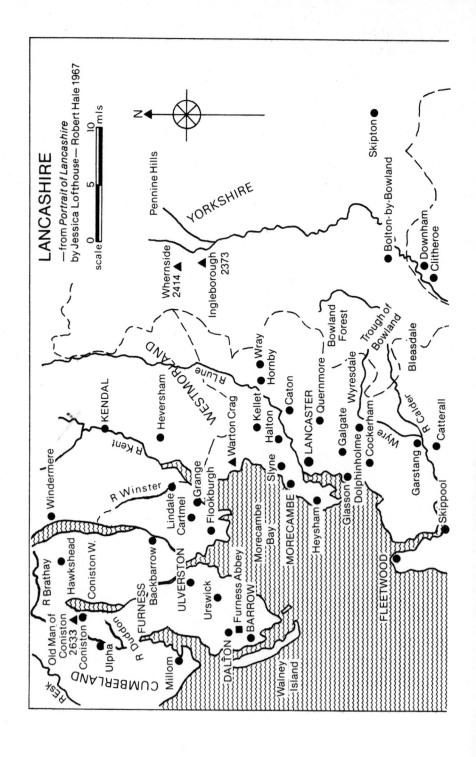

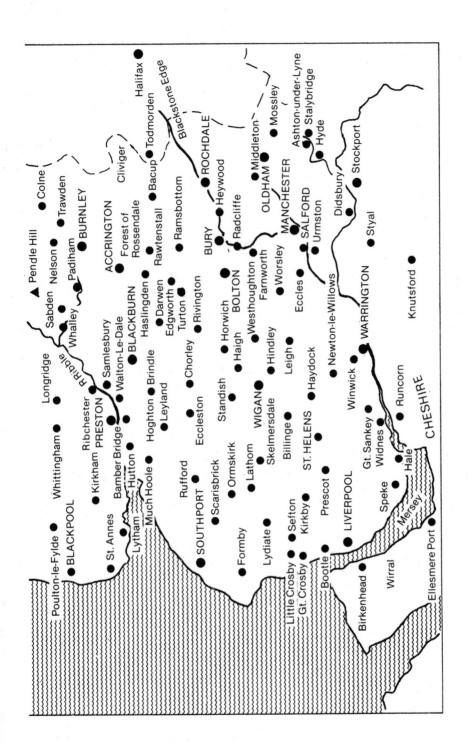

1 ORIGINS

This book is about life in the historic county of Lancaster, commonly called Lancashire — at least since the fifteenth century. Its boundaries became established under the Norman kings. These survived with only slight alteration for administrative and census purposes until 1 April 1974. On that date the old county boundaries were swept away by the Local Government Act, 1972, and the new truncated Lancashire emerged as merely the nucleus of the historic county.

In the north, North Lonsdale, including the towns of Ulverston and Barrow-in-Furness and the old Lancashire's highest point, the 2,631 feet (802 m) high peak of Coniston Old Man, all passed to the new county of Cumbria. In the south-west Liverpool, Southport, St Helens and the area between them became part of the new Merseyside Metropolitan County, while south-east Lancashire, including Wigan, Bolton, Bury, Rochdale and Salford all formed part of the Greater Manchester Metropolitan County. The river Mersey ceased to be the boundary between Lancashire and Cheshire. Warrington and Widnes now became part of the new Cheshire. The new Lancashire, centred on Preston, acquired parts of the former West Riding of Yorkshire, including the Forest of Bowland.

For our purposes, however, Lancashire denotes, as it did for eight centuries, the million or so acres stretching from the north side of Morecambe Bay to the north bank of the Mersey and from the Pennines to the Irish Sea. This area includes Walney Island and the Coniston fells in the extreme north and the Merseyside villages of Hale and Mossley in the extreme south.

The historic or ancient county, with these borders, came into existence in the reign of Henry II. Late in the twelfth century the

15

first sheriff was appointed to collect taxes for the whole county and the first assizes were held at Lancaster. Representatives of the shire were elected to attend Edward I's Model Parliament in 1296, along with those from the boroughs of Lancaster, Preston, Wigan and Liverpool. The earldom of Lancaster was created in 1266 for Henry III's youngest son, Edmund Crouchback, who was granted wide powers within the county outside the bounds of his own estates. In 1351 when Henry, the fourth earl, was given the title of duke, he was granted palatine powers for life by Edward III. This palatine authority gave Henry a position in Lancashire similar to that of the Earl of Chester or Bishop of Durham in their respective shires, namely the right to exercise almost royal powers in the appointment of judges and the holding of special duchy courts at Lancaster and Preston. The king's overall control was retained in his right to tax the county and to pardon those found guilty in the duke's courts. These palatine powers were resumed by the crown on Duke Henry's death in 1361, but they were also granted to his successor, John of Gaunt, in 1390. When he died in 1399, the duchy was seized by his nephew, Richard II. Gaunt's son, Henry Bolingbroke, returned from exile on the continent and wrested both duchy and kingdom from his cousin Richard, and was crowned Henry IV, first of the royal house of Lancaster.

The duchy was never again surrendered by the reigning monarch, and it survives to this day, in the form of crown lands and church patronage administered separately from those of other parts of the kingdom. The duchy council which had been peripatetic under John of Gaunt became stationary in London in the course of the fifteenth century. The court of the Duchy of Lancaster, headed by its own chancellor, administered the lands of the duchy, heard appeals from the chancery court at Preston and appointed the county's magistrates. Until 1873 the duchy was responsible for holding assizes in the county. Even today, the Chancellor of the Duchy of Lancaster, apart from being a government minister, carries out some of his traditional functions in that he appoints the judges and magistrates for Lancashire, Merseyside and Greater Manchester.

The first mention of the 'county of Lancaster' was in 1168. Lancaster was both the seat of the honour (or feudal lordship) and the assize town. Later it was at Lancaster that the magistrates of the county met in quarter sessions and where two knights of the shire were elected to attend the House of Commons at Westminster.

Lancaster's original advantage lay in its strategic position commanding the Lune Valley, one of the principal routes to Scotland. Its position weakened as the military importance of the castle declined and as the emergence of important centres of population to the south brought about a shift in the county's centre of gravity. In 1798 the headquarters of county government moved from Lancaster to Preston, and in 1835 additional assize courts were set up at Liverpool, and later at Manchester as well.

County government became less important to many Lancastrians in the late nineteenth century when a large number of towns achieved independence in the form of county borough status. Nevertheless Preston remained the seat of government for the smaller towns and the rural areas. In 1888 an elected county council replaced the general meeting of county magistrates which had previously governed the north-west. The system by which the county council governed rural areas and supervised some services to non-county boroughs survived until the reorganization in 1974. In that year the former county boroughs were incorporated in the new counties of Cumbria, Lancashire, Merseyside and Greater Manchester.

The origins of Lancashire lie in the remote past. About 500 million years ago, in what geologists call Ordovician times, the oldest rocks in the north-west, the Skiddaw Slates, were laid down. These were originally mudstones lying in various depths of water in a shallow sea off a large northern continent. In time the sea-bed became the scene of much volcanic activity which thrust up the main peaks of the Lake District, known as the Borrowdale Volcanic Series. The land was subject to a period of alternating sinkage and volcanic activity, giving rise to the Coniston limestone, grits and flags, which are the oldest rocks in north Lancashire. As the sea deepened a vast series of mudstones and silts, known as the Stockdale Series, accumulated.

For the development of Lancashire the most important period of rock formation took place about 350 million years ago when the sea once more covered the north-west and the Carboniferous limestone beds were laid down. It was this Carboniferous period which was largely responsible both for the structure of the landscape and the evolution of the regional economy. Limestone of this age may be seen near Clitheroe and Whalley. This sea-floor covering of limestone thickened with the years but, in turn, was subject to river deposits of sand and silt, which later hardened into the Millstone Grit Series

17

from which has been quarried much of the stone for building Lancaster and the Pennine villages. As these river deposits spread, the water became so shallow in places that swamp vegetation grew up, giving rise to the thin coal measures found occasionally in the Lancashire millstone grits, particularly in the form of moorland outcrops. In time, additional layers of sand and mud caused alternation of coal measures with strata of sandstones, grits and shales. In the nineteenth century the latter were exploited for brick-making, producing among other varieties, the famous bright red 'Accrington bloods'.

About 270 million years ago, in late Coal Measure times, the Carboniferous limestone underwent much folding. Such folds, with their axes running east–west, may be seen along the Pennine chain at various points. Folding was followed by erosion which wore away the summits of the limestone masses of Bowland and Rossendale.

The tectonic depression caused by the folding limestone attracted a variety of desert and inland-sea deposits in the Mesozoic period over 200 million years ago. This basin was filled up with a variety of Keuper marls (containing important salt deposits) and Bunter sandstones and conglomerates which now form the underlying Permo-Triassic rocks of the Lancashire plain. In south-west Lancashire they come close to the surface as a result of up-folding.

Much of this pre-glacial landscape was entirely altered by the Ice Age two million years ago. The ice sheet spread a thick layer of boulder clay and sand in the deeper valleys, diverting many streams from their original courses and coating the valley sides up to a height of 1,500 feet (450 m). Two levels of boulder clay have suggested two glacial advances. As the glaciers retreated, lakes were formed whose outlets later formed important means of communication between different valleys. An example is the Cliviger Gorge between Burnley and Todmorden. At Blackpool the boulder clay forms cliffs between 40 (12 m) and 70 feet (21 m) high. Where the drift has been eroded by streams on the edge of Rossendale, the coal outcrops have been exposed, as at Haigh and Blackrod.

The last two major geological developments were the alluvial deposits made by the rivers and the evolution of peatmosses. Flood gravels have allowed urban development in otherwise low-lying valley bottoms. Tidal action has formed the alluvial deposits into low coastal flats in the Fylde and west Lancashire. The fine sand of the Shirdley Hill variety has proved invaluable in the development of the glass industry at St Helens. The peatmosses, exploited for fuel long before coal, became established in various places, particularly along large stretches of the coast, on the north bank of the Mersey and in south-west Lancashire. Most of these areas have been drained in the last two or three hundred years.

Life began in the sea, which then covered most of Lancashire, about 450 million years ago. Fossil shells have been found in profusion in the Coniston Limestone Series, while remains of various fishes have been found in the coal measures dating back 300-400 million years. Mammals of late Pleistocene times, two or three million years ago, have been found at the mouths of the Ribble and the Mersey. In the late nineteenth century the skull of a brown bear was found at Bootle, and a variety of deer antlers were dredged from the Ribble during the excavation of Preston docks.

After the last Ice Age the climate became warmer and all but the highest ground in the county became covered with oak and birch forests. Into these forests, migrating northwards across the peat-mosses of the Mersey valley, came Lancashire's first human settlers. Penetration of the north-west seems to have occurred quite late, probably not before Mesolithic times (about 5,000 B.C.). The first men to reach Lancashire kept to the Pennine uplands where the forest was less thick, and so hunting and snaring were easier than in the wetter, deeper forest of the plain. Mesolithic man lived by fishing and hunting red deer, hares and wild boar, helped by his dogs. He ate the fish and meat, clothed himself in the hides and furs and used the deer antlers as tools which he later supplemented with stone or flint blades. Examples of such tools have come from near Bolton, Radcliffe and Anglezarke Moor near Rivington.

The Neolithic revolution brought agriculture to Europe. Neolithic man sowed seeds, cut grass with stone sickles and kept herds of cattle, sheep and goats. He began to clear the upland forest for himself and his animals. He made pottery, and his womenfolk wove cloth. In the north-west, Neolithic man continued to inhabit the moorland caves occupied by his predecessors, and Neolithic burial chambers have been found, like the one on Anglezarke Moor. But he also made a start on building dwellings of mud or wood, and some of the sites which he occupied were very low-lying, like Walney Island and Williamson's Moss. During Neolithic times a thriving trade in flints and stone axes developed. Flint-knapping sites have been found as far dispersed as Chorlton-on-Medlock, Clitheroe and Grange-over-Sands, while the stone axe 'factories' which supplied

19

the north-west and markets further afield were scattered through the Furness area and north Wales. There is also evidence of contact with Ireland, the Isle of Man and Yorkshire at this time.

Many of the practices of Neolithic man were unaltered by the coming of the Bronze Age. Some, however, changed. The Bronze Age coincided with a period of drier weather in the north-west, so substantial and waterproof dwellings were less essential. This at least is one explanation for the scarcity of known sites for this period. Stone circles of the Bronze Age may be seen at Bleasdale and on Turton Heights, while collared urn burials have been found at various places, including Whitelow near Bury. In 1973 a canoe burial of this period was uncovered by contractors near Jubilee Tower, Hare Appletree Fell near Lancaster. A hoard found at Portfield near Whalley revealed a number of bronze implements including two axes, a knife and a gouge, as well as some gold jewellery. This gold is likely to have been Irish in origin. About the same time the Ribble valley seems to have become an artery for the trade of flat bronze axes sent from Ireland to eastern England and even Scandinavia.

The Iron Age brought much wetter weather, and remains of this period are more substantial. A total of seven hill-forts have been traced in the county: at Camp Hill near Liverpool, Caster Cliff near Nelson, Portfield near Whalley, Castlestede near Lancaster, Warton Crag, Castlehead near Lindale and Skelmore Heads near Ulverston. There is a noticeable concentration of these hill-forts in Lonsdale, and to the four in this area might be added Ingleborough in the Lune valley, perhaps a regional capital of the Brigantes, the tribe which dominated the north immediately before the Roman conquest. The largest of the Lancashire forts is Warton Crag, which extends over 15 acres (6 ha). The rest were small. Hut settlements too have been found. Using stone foundations, Iron Age man built circular huts roofed with branches covered with skins or thatch. Each settlement was probably for one extended family. At Urswick the hut circles measure over 20 feet (6 m) in diameter and are surrounded by rectangular cattle paddocks. Elsewhere, terracing shows the sites of Celtic fields.

2 THE ROMAN OCCUPATION

It was not until 30 years after the invasion of Britain by the Emperor Claudius that the conquest of the Lancashire area was undertaken by the Romans. The civil war of A.D. 69 in Italy encouraged a palace revolution among the Brigantes, in which the pro-Roman queen, Cartimandua, was driven out by her former husband, Venutius. The Romans quickly recovered from the civil war, once Vespasian had emerged as the new emperor, and two expeditions were sent against the Brigantes. The first, under Petilius Cerialis, broke the backbone of Brigantian resistance in the campaigns of 71-4. The second, led by Gnaeus Julius Agricola, took place in 78-9, when the latter, who had been Cerialis' lieutenant on the earlier occasion, returned to Britain as governor and completed the conquest of the north.

Although the details of Agricola's campaign are not fully known, his route seems to have followed the western foothills of the Pennines, with diversions to explore the forests and estuaries. His 'base line' was the axial road linking the two new legionary fortresses of Chester and York. In preparation for the campaign, Agricola had moved Legion XX *Valeria Victrix* from Wroxeter to Chester and had already led it to victory in north Wales. The starting-point for the Roman campaign in the north-west was probably Chester, but a timber auxiliary fort may already have been established at Manchester (Mamucium), on the road between Chester and York. Historians assume that Agricola's line of march roughly followed the first Roman road to be built through the north-west which ran north out of Manchester (along the modern A58), crossing the Irwell at Radcliffe, through Edgworth and Blackburn, to the Ribble crossing

21

at Ribchester (Bremetennacum), a total distance of about 25 miles (40 km). This was further than the Romans normally marched in a day, but no other camps have been found in the area. At Ribchester a temporary turf fort was erected in the typical Roman manner: a double ditch, the inside bank of which was reinforced with bricks of turf bonded with layers of brushwood. On the top of the bank the soldiers would have put up a fence of stakes, usually about seven feet long, placed about six inches apart and tied together in the middle. North of Ribchester, on Mellor Hill, a signalling station was set up at a strategic point for the Ribble valley and Aire Gap route through the Pennines. There are remains of another Agricolan turf camp at Carr Hill, just outside Kirkham and 15 miles (24 km) west of Ribchester. From here, the general could have contacted the fleet, which probably accompanied him northwards. Later the Romans built a road, known as the Danes Pad, north-west from Kirkham. Perhaps somewhere on the Wyre estuary lie the remains of the port of the Setantii, mentioned on Ptolemy's famous map, but as yet undiscovered. The Danes Pad has been traced as far as Hardhorn, and one suggestion has been that its destination was Skippool.

Agricola's main thrust was northwards from Ribchester over the Trough of Bowland and up to Burrow-in-Lonsdale (Galacum). Early Flavian remains at Lancaster suggest, however, another diversion, once again to the estuary of a major river — this time the Lune — where the general could renew contact with his fleet. The next Agricolan fort was that of Burrow-in-Lonsdale, from where he continued north, to Watercrook, near Kendal, by-passing Furness. Such a programme is a matter of conjecture, but, at the very least, archaeological evidence tells us that penetration to the west coast from the line of forts in the Pennine foothills rapidly followed the initial advance.

A second north-south route was made 20 years after Agricola's first conquest of the north-west. Usually referred to as the coastal route, this road ran north through the Lancashire plain and was probably built to provide a service link to the frontier in lowland Scotland. It ran from Middlewich and Northwich in Cheshire and crossed the river Mersey at Wilderspool, opposite modern Warrington. From Wilderspool the road passed northward through Winwick and Wargrave to Wigan (perhaps the site of Coccium), crossed the river Ribble at Walton-le-Dale, and thence proceeded north to Lancaster

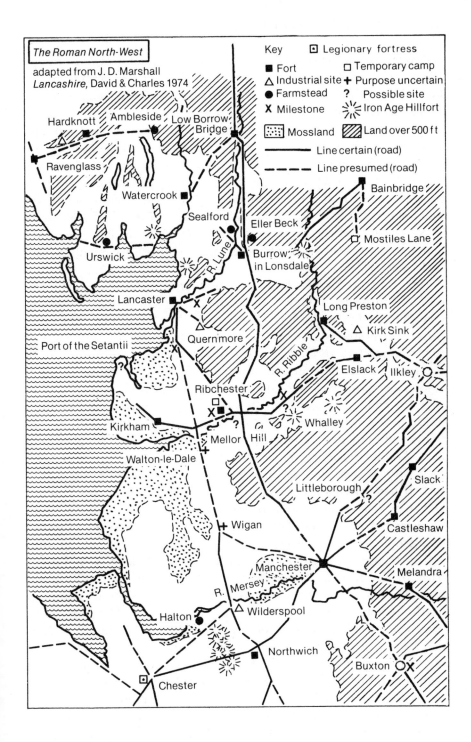

The Roman North-West

adapted from J. D. Marshall
Lancashire, David & Charles 1974

Key

■· Legionary fortress
■ Fort
△ Industrial site
● Farmstead
X Milestone
□ Temporary camp
+ Purpose uncertain
? Possible site
※ Iron Age Hillfort
▓ Mossland
▨ Land over 500 ft
—— Line certain (road)
‑‑‑ Line presumed (road)

Hardknott
Ambleside
Low Borrow Bridge
Ravenglass
Watercrook
Sealford
Eller Beck
Bainbridge
Mostiles Lane
Urswick
Burrow in Lonsdale
R. Lune
Lancaster
Long Preston
Kirk Sink
Quernmore
Port of the Setantii
R. Ribble
Elslack
Ilkley
Ribchester
Whalley
Kirkham
Mellor Hill
Slack
Walton-le-Dale
Littleborough
Wigan
Castleshaw
Manchester
Melandra
R. Mersey
Halton
Wilderspool
Northwich
Buxton
Chester

23

and Watercrook. This road was part of Route 10 on the Antonine Itinerary, and was a great addition to Chester's communications, as well as providing better means of policing the Lancashire plain.

As already mentioned Agricola sited the legionary fort for the north-west at Chester, where it could be provisioned and relieved, if occasion demanded, by sea, and from where it could keep a close watch on the mountains of Wales as well as the western Brigantes. A string of auxiliary forts was established in Lancashire, and they provide us with the main evidence of Roman occupation. Later buildings have made the excavation of many of these difficult. Even at Ribchester, where a series of excavations since the late nineteenth century has revealed a great deal, many of the fort details remain uncertain.

According to Mr Ben Edwards, the county archaeologist, the lay-out of Ribchester followed the standard pattern of many auxiliary forts. Originally built of turf and wood, like the other Lancashire forts, Ribchester was soon rebuilt in stone. The chief building was the headquarters (*principia*). This was situated at the centre where the roads from the four gateways crossed. It consisted of the usual colonnaded drill hall and chapel for the regimental standards, built round a courtyard containing a well. Nearby was the commander's house (*praetorium*), and to the north were the granaries, with flagged floors and timber roofs, where the regiment's vital food supplies were kept. Around the perimeter were the barrack blocks, grouped in pairs, each with its own veranda. The bath-house was situated outside the fort. It had a boiler-house and four rooms (cold, warm, hot and hot and dry). The three heated rooms were connected to a boiler-room by means of stoke-holes and flues. Other finds suggest the existence of a temple for the garrison.

The troops stationed in the Lancashire forts came from various parts of the Roman Empire. Very few came from Italy. Ribchester was garrisoned at different times by cavalry units from Asturia in north Spain and from Sarmatia on the Danube. The Sarmatians were sent to Ribchester by the Emperor Marcus Aurelius in 175, as part of a plan to strengthen the frontiers of the empire. Manchester was at one time garrisoned by Rhaetians from Switzerland and Noricans from the Tyrol. At Lancaster there was a cavalry unit of Sebosians from Gaul. Gravestones from Ribchester and Lancaster show that the north-west was manned by soldiers from as far afield as Trier on the Rhine, Asia Minor and Portugal.

24

Civilian settlements (*vici*) were attached to each fort. Judging by the excavations at Manchester and Ribchester, these grew up on the roads leading to the main gates of the fort. The presence of the soldiers attracted a variety of services. Some of the shops in Church Street, Lancaster, have Roman foundations. At Ribchester there was ribbon development of single-storey, timber-frame buildings stretching northwards. The timber-framing was primitive. The uprights were merely driven into the ground. The walls were of wattle and daub, the floors of clay, covered with straw. To judge from these buildings the civilians at Ribchester obviously did not grow particularly rich from the trade provided by the fort, or perhaps the houses were for the wives and relatives of the soldiers. From the gaming counters, knucklebones and broken *amphorae* (wine-bottles) found near the east gate of the fort at Manchester, it is clear that an inn or gambling-house was situated there. Such a *vicus* as Manchester would have been largely self-sufficient except in wine, Samian pottery and other luxuries.

Some settlements were purely commercial. Walton-le-Dale and Wilderspool were in this category. Although some maps suggest that there was a fortlet at Walton-le-Dale, no hint of military occupation has ever been found there. Wilderspool — strictly in Cheshire but undoubtedly supplying much of south Lancashire in Roman times — has revealed some of the most spectacular finds in the north-west. From its foundation in about 85, the community was industrial. Furnaces indicate glass-making and metal-smelting of various kinds, principally of iron objects for agriculture and hunting purposes, such as axes, sickles, mattocks and arrowheads. Pottery and tiles were manufactured on an extensive scale, as were enamel brooches and glass beads, which doubtless became gifts to soldiers' wives and British women. An example of a smaller industrial site is the pottery at Quernmore, where a potter by the name of Tritus supplied the garrison and fort at Lancaster.

In the countryside the patterns of farming established in the Iron Age continued virtually unchanged. The cattle and horse breeders of the Pennines still lived in their stone huts, with walled enclosures nearby for their beasts. Contact with the Romans would have been slight. Beyond collecting taxes — probably in the form of hides — the Romans did not interfere much in the life of these hill farmers. Yet three centuries of Roman occupation did not leave them completely untouched. They undoubtedly benefited from the roads which they helped to build, and by the second century A.D. there was a whole network of minor roads, quite apart from the main routes. The towns attached to the forts gave them opportunities to sell their cattle products and their horses. One theory, based on bone remains, is that a larger breed of horse was introduced into the north-west as a result of this trade between soldiers and civilians. Finds of coins and pottery in their villages imply that the hill-farmers bought some of the new wares available at places like Wilderspool.

The existence of religious cults popular with the troops is clear from historic evidence at Hulme (Manchester) and Wigan, and from the lamp inscribed with the Christian 'chi-rho' monogram at Lancaster. The Manchester cryptogram (ROTAS OPERA TENET AREPO SATOR) decoded as PATER NOSTER, dates from the second century and may provide the earliest evidence of Christianity in Britain.

The Romans were not particularly interested in improving the agriculture of the north-west as a whole, but it is quite likely that veterans from the forts settled in the neighbouring districts. Some of this settlement was probably on virgin land, and it is believed by some scholars that Roman veterans were among the first to start draining and cultivating the Fylde. One tends to associate the Romans with arable cultivation, but there is no reason why the settlers in the north-west may not have taken up cattle-farming like the Britons. The valleys of the Lune and Ribble may well have seen villa-type settlement, although as yet, no Roman villa has been identified in the county. Of possible sites, one of the most likely is Folly Farm, near Lancaster, where an altar has been found dedicated by a retired cavalry officer, Julius Januarius, to a local Celtic god, Romanized as Jalonus Contrebis. Contrebis was the Roman name for Lunesdale.

How far the Romans brought law and order to the north-west is debatable. Their forts were scattered throughout the region, and a good road system allowed for ease of access. Nevertheless, some areas remained remote and were possibly always subject to looting and cattle-rustling, even at the height of Roman rule in the second century. The Roman garrisons were not withdrawn until about 400. Yet, even before then, life had undergone major disruptions in the third and fourth centuries. Southern Scotland was no longer occupied by the Romans at the end of the second century, so restoring to the north of England the frontier zone status of earlier times.

Three major incursions by the Picts occurred in 196, 296 and 367, and there were prolonged periods of civil war. The north-west no doubt benefited from the protection given by the Pennines, but many Picts attacked from the sea, and Lancashire would have suffered from a second scourge — raiding parties from Ireland. The redevelopment of Lancaster as a shore fort in the fourth century provided only temporary relief, dependent on the effectiveness of a fleet or coastguard system.

Once the migration of the fourth and fifth centuries had got under way, there was little that Roman soldiers or walls could do to stop them. After the disasters of 196, 296 and 367, the forts were repaired and order restored, but the security of the second century was never to be regained. Many of the Roman sites have suggested a violent end — usually destruction by fire — followed by abandonment. When did the end come? Troops were withdrawn by usurping generals in 383, 402 and 407. In 410, the Emperor Honorius ordered British towns to organize their own defences against the barbarians. In Lancashire the Pictish and Scottish raids probably became fiercer and more penetrating. The archaeological sites have so far revealed less about the end of the Roman military occupation than we could wish. Roman Lancashire was subject to periodic raids from the late second century onwards. Some sites were re-occupied after destruction, others were not. Although civilian settlements like Walton-le-Dale and Wilderspool suffered from the disruptions of the late second century, there are signs that economic life resumed there in the third. The fort of Kirkham was no longer garrisoned after the second century, but Ribchester, Lancaster and Watercrook were all occupied by troops until the late fourth century, as was the legionary fortress of Chester. Lancaster, like Chester, was rebuilt in the fourth century, to which the so-called 'Wery Wall' still stands testimony at the top of Vicarage Fields. The fort's reconstruction seems to have been a western continuation of the line of coastal defences known as the forts of the Saxon shore, and it probably served as a base for the Roman fleet as it kept a look-out for the flotillas of the Pictish and Scottish raiders. Without the fleet and without a garrison, such shore forts became useless. Lancaster probably survived no better than Pevensey (Anderida) in Sussex, where the Saxons won a major victory in 491.

How much the Britons continued to live in the townships formerly sheltered by these forts is hard to say. The economic life which the

Roman military occupation had fostered declined when its presence was removed. Lancashire may well have suffered, like other parts of the empire, from plague and famine as well as war, all tending towards a reduction of the population. In such circumstances one would expect reversion to the scattered British farmsteads. There can be no certainty in such speculation. The initial attraction of the forts and their adjacent townships as places rich in booty must soon have faded from over-exploitation, and life perhaps carried on among the ruins of past military grandeur. When the raiders came to settle, they tended to establish colonies in new places away from Roman or Romano-British occupation. This may have been an additional incentive to continue in the older communities. If so, they were small and life was at a much more primitive level. The little archaeological evidence that there is suggests the abandonment of any attempt at Roman standards of living.

3 SAXONS
AND VIKINGS

Archaeologists assure us that the post-Roman period was not as dark as was once thought. We are now told that the material decline, which resulted from the collapse of Roman commerce, was accompanied by a religious revival, as Christianity — not always of an orthodox kind — became a force which helped to unite the British against the Saxon invaders. At the same time, the conversion of the Irish by British missionaries helped to create a new Celtic culture centred round the Irish Sea, characterized by superlative metalwork and a revival in trade with the continent.

The stories of Arthur also suggest that the north-west was not entirely abandoned to either Picts, Scots or Saxons. This is hardly surprising, because the north-west lay between such major centres of British survival as the kingdom of Elmet in the Yorkshire dales and the kingdom of Maelgwn in north Wales. Arthur is supposed to have won a battle near Chester (the City of the Legion in Arthurian tales). Although William Camden's claim in *Britannia* (1582) that the river Douglas was the site of several other British victories is not upheld by modern scholars, other battles with the invaders are thought to have been fought in the neighbourhood of Carlisle and the Scottish lowlands. If so, British predominance in the north-west was probably maintained, in spite of some Angle and Saxon penetration, until the end of the sixth century.

West of the Pennines was territory disputed between the British kingdoms which emerged from the wreck of the Roman Empire. For a time it belonged to a north Welsh kingdom called Teyrnllwg. British hegemony, however, was destroyed at the battle of Chester, *circa* 615, when an alliance of the Christian Celts was broken by the pagan Saxon, Ethelfrith, king of Northumbria, who drove the British back into the fastnesses of north Wales. Thereafter, the area subsequently known as Lancashire was disputed between the Saxon kingdoms of Northumbria, to the east, and Mercia, to the south. Ecclesiastical boundaries suggest that the river Ribble became the dividing line between their two spheres of influence. This division of the north-west is thought to have lasted from the seventh to the ninth centuries, when both Mercia and Northumbria fell victim, along with East Anglia, to the campaign of 'the Great Army' of the Danes in the years 865-80. Mercia recovered under the leadership of the kings of Wessex after 900, but Northumbria, like East Anglia, remained under the Danelaw of Danish rule, as established by the treaty of Wedmore between Alfred, king of Wessex, and the Danish leader, Guthrum, in 878.

The Angles and Saxons seem first to have penetrated into Lancashire in the late sixth century. Anglo-Saxon place-names ending with '-ingas' and '-inghaham' ('-'s people' and '-'s people's home') are the principal evidence for this. Such place endings are rare in Lanchashire compared to the south and east of England, and the origins of such places as Whittingham (Hwita's people's home) and Padiham (Pada's people's home) seem to lie in the migration of small groups of Angles and Saxons across the Pennine valleys in the late sixth and early seventh centuries. Men like Hwita and Pada would have been chiefs or leaders, who broke off from the main bands of settlers on the east coast and moved inland as a kind of advance party or pioneer group.

We can only guess at their way of life from scattered pieces of archaeological evidence from Lancashire itself and what we know of their better documented and researched contemporaries of eastern England. There is no reason to suppose that they were very different from the men described in the epic poem *Beowulf*, even though their route into Lancashire took them a long way from the sea. If Beowulf described much of what was found at Sutton Hoo in Suffolk in 1939, it must not be forgotten that the river Douglas also yielded an early Saxon barrow during excavations by navvies in 1770. Described as 'British' the finds were probably Saxon:

In the knoll there were found numerous fragments of iron, various military weapons, such as our ancestors buried in the graves of their heroes, and, under all, a cavity of seven feet in length, filled with black earth and the decomposed remains of one of the fallen chieftains.

Most of the Saxon settlers seem to have reached the north-west overland, but possibly some came by sea, and some certainly settled by the coast, even though much of the Lancashire coastal plain was still either swamp or sandy waste. It has been pointed out that the earliest arrivals seem to have settled the higher land, while later ones had to make do with marshier ground. Among latecomers we may include the Norse settlers of the tenth century. The Saxons avoided both the peatmosses and the barren fells. From evidence of place-names and the *Domesday Book*, their settlements were concentrated at altitudes between 100 feet (30 m) and 800 feet (245 m) above sea level.

The fate of the existing Romano-British inhabitants of Lancashire is difficult to ascertain. Place-names can only tell us so much. Absorption of the natives by the newcomers seems to have been the typical pattern, though the process may have taken centuries to complete. The area was sparsely populated, and Saxon migrants could easily find uninhabited parts in which to settle. The gradual spread of technical improvements such as the iron plough share, which had been introduced to Britain in Roman times, enabled a more extensive cultivation of valley land and the clearance of forests where wolves, boars and wild cats still roamed. By the seventh century, some cultivation of new land was being undertaken by the monasteries. Whalley, for example, belonged to a cell of Celtic monks, who perhaps formed part of that Irish-dominated culture mentioned above. About 660 they were driven out by the Northumbrians, who gave their lands to the monastery at Ripon, newly founded according to the Benedictine Rule by St Wilfrid. That some British settlements survived undisturbed is suggested by the number of places still called by the Saxon name of Walton, meaning 'the settlement of the British'.

Town life, which had been introduced by the Romans and was largely concentrated around their forts, probably died out after the Roman withdrawal. At Manchester, the Roman fort and the early Saxon fortifications, known later as the Hanging Ditch, are not on the same site, suggesting no continuity of settlement. As Dr J.D. Bu'lock has written in Jones and Grealey, *Roman Manchester* (1974):

For post-Roman Manchester the local resources were the woods, with wild game and domestic pigs, the river for fishing, and a very modest area of tillage. The most permanent vestiges of Roman Manchester were to be the line of highway which is modern Deansgate and the location of the river crossings which it defines, by Knott Mill on the Medlock and at Hunts Bank, under Victoria Station, on the Irk.

The disturbed border with its thin population discouraged town life. The Saxons of Mercia and Northumbria regarded the north-west as a no-man's-land to be colonized only by the hardiest of settlers.

In the tenth century, it was the Saxons of Wessex, following King Alfred's victories over the Danes, who made the greatest impact on the north-west. When Edward the Elder, son of King Alfred and King of Wessex 901-25, was securing his position against the Danes, he set up a line of forts, in conjunction with his sister Aethelflaed, to guard the line of the Mersey. The fortifications of Chester were repaired in 907, and new forts were built at Eddisbury (914), Runcorn (915) and Thelwall (919). (In *Warrington and the Mid-Mersey Valley* (1971), Mr G.A. Carter suggests that this fort may have commanded the river-crossing, in which case the site of modern Warrington is more likely than that of modern Thelwall.) Manchester's earlier Saxon earthworks were restored in 922, thus completing the line from Chester to the Pennines and defending north-west Mercia from attack.

There was no such strong power to defend the lands north of the Mersey, and they may well have been a battleground for the Norsemen, the Danes and the men of Strathclyde. The insecurity of the north-west is indicated only by one or two snippets of information available from charters, chronicles and archaeological finds, which tend to pose more questions than they answer. Why did Tilred, abbot of Heversham, transfer to the abbey of Norham-on-Tweed in the early tenth century? Who buried the Cuerdale (Preston) and Harkirke (Crosby) hoards of the same period and why? In this period of disturbance and confusion there is little reassurance in the submissions which Wessex kings, Edward the Elder, Athelstan and Edgar received from the kings of Strathclyde and from Danish leaders periodically throughout the tenth century, in their efforts to establish hegemony over all England. The very need for such submissions suggests political upheaval and instability in the north-west.

The most famous battle between the Saxons and their enemies

in this period was that fought at Brunanburh in 937, when Athelstan, King of Wessex, defeated a coalition of Scots and Norsemen. One theory claims that Brunanburh was fought at Saxifield, near Burnley, but others argue for sites as far distant as Beverley or on the Solway. There is no conclusive evidence for any site, but the *Anglo-Saxon Chronicle* describes the kind of battle that must have been fought on north-western soil in this period. Brunanburh was such a massacre that 'the field grew dark with the blood of men'.

> . . .Five young kings,
> Stretched lifeless by the swords,
> Lay on the field, likewise seven
> Of Anlaf's jarls and a countless host
> Of seamen and Scots.

Anlaf, King of the Norsemen, and Constantine, King of the Scots, were both put to flight, while Athelstan and his brother Edmund returned to Wessex leaving behind:

> The horn-beaked raven with dusky plumage,
> And the hungry hawk of battle, the dun-coated
> Eagle, who with white-tipped tail shared
> The feast with the wolf, grey beast of the forest.

The result of the battle was that Athelstan became the undisputed overlord of the English and moved his northern frontier from the Mersey to the Ribble, keeping the intervening land under his own control.

Scandinavian settlement in the north-west, both north and south of the Ribble, was already a *fait accompli* by the time of Athelstan's victory. The Scandinavians approached the area from two directions: the Danes from the east Midlands, the Norwegians from Ireland and the Isle of Man. Danish settlement of places like Oldham, Hulme and Urmston, in south-east Lancashire, was the result of the inroads made by the Great Army in the late ninth century. Norse colonization was rather different. Their arrival in the early tenth century has been described as infiltration rather than invasion. The *Anglo-Saxon Chronicle* states that the Norsemen were driven from Dublin in 902 (the year after King Alfred's death) and settled on the Wirral, near Chester, soon afterwards. This first appearance of Norsemen as settlers was followed by many others further up the coast, for the Lancashire seaboard from Aigburth on the Mersey to Flookburgh in Furness is thick with place-names of Norse origin. Many of these are found on the low-lying land which the Saxons had apparently rejected.

Norsemen and Danes alike founded a great number of island settlements, such as Ormskirk and Burscough in south-west Lancashire and the '-hulme' settlements to the east. Oldham, according to Ekwall, was situated in the old district of Kaskenmoor (the moor of sedge grass), and in its original form of Aldholm or Aldhulm, referred to 'a piece of dry land in mossland'. Both Norsemen and Danes spread along the river-valleys where they had first settled. The former's place-names occur in the valleys of the rivers Douglas, Wyre, Lune and Leven.

Mention of this infiltration is rare in contemporary documents. One twelfth century charter makes passing reference to the Norse settlers of Amounderness (headland of Agmund) in that about 930, King Athelstan granted to the church of York: 'all of Agmunderness, which he had bought from the heathen'.

By the mid-tenth century Lancashire had become a great hotch-potch of different peoples, languages and religious traditions. The agricultural system continued to be based primarily on cattle in the upland areas, but on the plain, among the peatmosses, considerable progress in arable cultivation was made. The family remained the principal social unit, even though a good deal of the settlement of Saxons, Danes and Norsemen was in groups of families, often forming small nucleated communities. Large areas of the north-west still remained bleak and intractable, but the framework for future settlement had been laid.

In spite of political uncertainty and social confusion, the north-west underwent a steady, although not always permanent, conversion to Christianity. Archaeological remains of the Roman period show that Lancashire was already touched by the Christian religion. It is easier to measure the extent of Christian influence in post-Roman times when Celtic monasteries flourished at Bangor-on-Dee and at Whalley. Place-names incorporating 'eccles' (from the Latin *ecclesia*, a church) such as Eccles and Eccleston indicate the whereabouts of some Celtic churches.

The territorial expansion of the Saxons in the late sixth century, and their official conversion to Christianity in the early seventh century, ended the separate life of the Celtic Church in the north-west. The region was first designated part of Paulinus's diocese in

625, and later came under the missionary influence of the North-umbrians — hence the dedication of churches to St Oswald at Winwick, St Chad at Poulton-le-Fylde, St Cuthbert at Lytham, and St Wilfrid at Preston and Halton. Although it is doubtful whether, as tradition has it, these were actually founded by their patron saints, Wilfrid's abbey at Ripon did acquire land west of the Pennines, and mission-ary activities by Wilfrid and Cuthbert cannot be ruled out. In spite of the Danish and Norse attacks of the late ninth and early tenth cen-turies, the links with Northumbria continued, and when the bound-aries of the dioceses were decided, land north of the Ribble went to York, while that to the south became the responsibility of the Mercian diocese of Lichfield.

Lancashire churchyard crosses show the mingled influences of Northumbria and Norse folk-lore, perhaps indicating that the Saxon and Norse communities were settling down together. Scholars have identified a similarity between Lancashire crosses and those of the schools of sculpture of Hexham and Ripon. The assimilation of Norse folk-lore into the dominant Saxon Christian tradition can be seen at Halton and Heysham. The shaft of the Halton cross shows both the Crucifixion and the Sigurd Saga, while at Heysham a hog-back tombstone bears on one side the victory of Christ over death and on the other, a representation of Ragnarok or the destruction of the Norse heaven. Cultural fusion was already well under way by the time the Norman invasion of 1066 brought to the north-west a new ruling class and unified, for administrative purposes, lands north and south of the Ribble.

4 MEDIAEVAL LANCASHIRE

Although Lancashire did not yet exist as a separate entity, the north-west played some part in the changes which overtook the English state in the second half of the eleventh century. North of the Ribble formed part of the huge earldom of Northumbria, which, in 1055, was given to Tostig, third son of the powerful Earl Godwin. Tostig had many enemies and twice had to escape abroad. During his second exile his half-brother, Harold, was chosen king by the Witan, or royal council, on Edward the Confessor's death, and Tostig made an alliance against his brother with King Harald Hardrada of Norway. They landed in Yorkshire, but their combined force of Northumbrians and Norwegians was defeated by Harold at the battle of Stamford Bridge. Tostig himself was killed. Immediately after the battle Harold's army had to rush south to cope with an invading force led by Duke William of Normandy. The two armies met at Hastings; this time it was Harold who was defeated and killed.

The Norman Conquest of England was accomplished swiftly and with a minimum of bloodshed. One area where resistance lasted longer than in most of the country was Northumbria. The Northern Revolt of 1069 was ruthlessly crushed, and Amounderness seems to have suffered along with the vale of York. Later, William gave the lands previously held by Earl Tostig to one of his followers, Roger of Poitou. As well as Amounderness, Roger was given the lands *'inter Ripam et Mersham'* (between Ribble and Mersey), and Roger chose Penwortham on the Ribble estuary, as the site for his castle. After the Conqueror's death in 1087, Roger helped the new king, William Rufus, against his brother Duke Robert, and, in 1092, against Dolfin, a rebel border-lord in the neighbourhood of Carlisle.

After a successful campaign against Dolfin and the Scots, Rufus gave Roger extensive territories in the borderlands between Northumbria and Strathclyde. Thus for the first time since the Romans, the lands on both banks of the Ribble were to be administered as one unit. Even so the Ribble remained an ecclesiastical boundary until 1541, and was a border for probate purposes until 1858.

Roger took the title of 'count' in 1091, when he succeeded to large estates in Poitou. Although he built a castle at Lancaster, inside the remains of the Roman fort, and made this the chief place in his honour, he never bore the title of 'Count of Lancaster'. Count Roger had been loyal to William Rufus, but rebelled against Henry I in 1102 and consequently lost his English estates. Such was the importance of this large frontier fief that Norman kings never allowed it out of their hands for long. In 1117 Henry I granted Lancaster to his nephew, Stephen, whom he made Count of Mortain. Stephen held onto the honour when he became king in 1135, but in the wars which followed, Lancashire came under the control of King David of Scotland.

With the deaths of David and Stephen in 1153 and 1154, the new kings of England and Scotland came to a deal whereby Henry II ruled south of the Ribble and Malcolm the Maiden north of it. By 1157, however, Henry II had gained all that Stephen had lost, and for most of his reign kept Lancaster as part of the royal demesne or estates. His successor, Richard the Lionheart, entrusted the northwest to his brother, John. John rebuilt the castle and granted a charter to the borough of Lancaster, but forfeited the honour for treason in 1194, and it remained with the crown until 1267. As king, John did much for the honour of Lancaster, and although there are mentions of the 'county' of Lancaster as early as the Pipe Rolls of 1168-9, it was not until his reign (1199-1216) that the organization of its fiscal and judicial administration may be regarded as complete.

What was Lancashire like at this time? Our knowledge — albeit sketchy — stems from William the Conqueror's desire to discover details of his new kingdom and the Domesday Survey of 1086, which he initiated. The chronicler at Peterborough described what happened:

He (William) sent his men all over England into every shire to ascertain how many hundreds of hides of land there were in each shire, and how much land and livestock the king owned in the country, and what annual dues were lawfully his from each shire. He also had it recorded how much land his archbishops had, and his diocesan bishops, his abbots and his earls, and . . . how much each man who was a land-holder here in England had in land or in livestock, and how much money it was worth.

The Peterborough Chronicle

The survey was made by special commissioners who derived their information from local juries made up of a cross-section of the rural population, often including the sheriff, lord of the manor, parish priest, local reeve or steward, and villeins.

In *Great Domesday* (the first volume of the *Domesday Book*), Lancashire south of the Ribble is to be found with the Cheshire folios, while north Lancashire and adjacent parts of Cumberland and Westmorland were regarded as simply a north-western appendage of Eurvicscire or Yorkshire.

The commissioners found six hundreds or wapentakes south of the Ribble: West Derby, Newton, Warrington, Salford, Blackburn and Leyland. Most of this land had belonged to King Edward the Confessor in 1066, and five of the six hundredal divisions coincided with royal manors. Each hundred was named after the administrative centre of the manor — perhaps no more than a hall where the king's reeve held the manor court, but which all the king's tenants had to attend from time to time.

Detailed accounts of landholdings in Lancashire in 1086 are only available for the hundred of West Derby and for some vills or townships north of the Ribble, such as Preston and Halton. A typical entry is that for Lydiate in West Derby: 'Uctred held Lydiate. There, six bovates of land. A wood, one league long and two furlongs broad. It was worth 64d.' Elsewhere the surveyors lumped all the vills together and gave a total for the manor. The manor of Leyland is an example: 'King Edward held Lailand. There are one hide and two carucates of land . . . . To this manor belonged twelve carucates of land which twelve freemen held for as many manors. In these are six hides and eight carucates of land'. Areas of woodland were separately mentioned. Unfortunately it is impossible to convert these measurements accurately into acres or hectares. All we know is that a bovate, or oxgang, was originally the area which could be ploughed by a single ox, while the carucate was supposed to be the

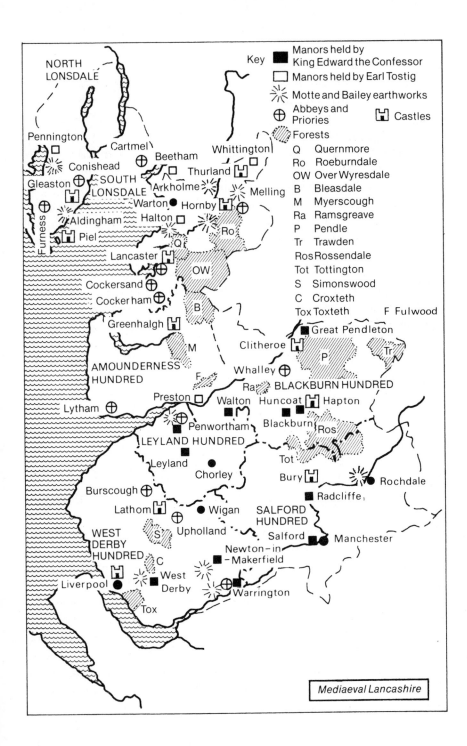

Key
■ Manors held by King Edward the Confessor
□ Manors held by Earl Tostig
☼ Motte and Bailey earthworks
⊕ Abbeys and Priories
🏰 Castles
▨ Forests

Q   Quernmore
Ro   Roeburndale
OW   Over Wyresdale
B   Bleasdale
M   Myerscough
Ra   Ramsgreave
P   Pendle
Tr   Trawden
Ros Rossendale
Tot Tottington
S   Simonswood
C   Croxteth
Tox Toxteth
F   Fulwood

NORTH LONSDALE
Pennington
Cartmel
Beetham
Whittington
Thurland
SOUTH LONSDALE
Arkholme
Gleaston
Conishead
Warton
Hornby
Melling
Furness
Aldingham
Halton
Piel
Ro
Q
Lancaster
OW
Cockersand
Cockerham
B
Greenhalgh
M
Great Pendleton
Clitheroe
P
Tr
AMOUNDERNESS HUNDRED
F
Whalley
Ra
BLACKBURN HUNDRED
Lytham
Preston
Walton
Huncoat
Hapton
Penwortham
Blackburn
Ros
LEYLAND HUNDRED
Leyland
Chorley
Tot
Bury
Rochdale
Burscough
Radcliffe
Lathom
Wigan
SALFORD HUNDRED
S
Upholland
Salford
Manchester
WEST DERBY HUNDRED
C
Newton-in-Makerfield
Liverpool
West Derby
Warrington
Tox

Mediaeval Lancashire

area ploughable by eight oxen in a morning.

The *Domesday Book* and later sources give some picture of the Lancashire countryside in the second half of the eleventh century. A great deal of it was still composed of peatmoss and woodland. Dr J.J. Bagley has computed that even in West Derby, the most cultivated of all the hundreds, there was as much woodland as arable land and the peatmosses accounted for five times the area covered by arable and wooded land together. While the mosses were to be found largely on the western side towards the sea and in the valley of the Mersey, the woodlands formed parallel belts from Liverpool to Lathom, along the Billinge-Upholland ridge, and from Bolton north-westwards as far as Walton-le-Dale. North of the Ribble the fells were covered with woodland, and most of the settlement was in the upper reaches of the rivers Lune, Kent and Leven.

The frequent reference to plough-teams in the Domesday Survey confirms that much of the cleared land was arable. The clerks felt that one plough-team should be expected for every plough-land, but in Lancashire there were rarely so many. The fringes of the woodlands provided acorns and beechmast for pigs. In the depths of the forest there were valuable 'eyries' or hawks' nests for rearing young birds of prey, and 'hays' or enclosures for trapping deer. The rivers provided fish, although only the fishery at Penwortham is mentioned. The mosses provided peat for fuel and osiers for basket work. Dr I.B. Terrett in *The Domesday Geography of Northern England* (1962) has concluded that although 'clearly a poor area', the north-west had a surprising number of settlements. Altogether the value of the six hundreds south of the Ribble in 1066 was given as £145 2s 2d. Twenty years after, the values had changed little. North of the Ribble had not fared so well, for only 16 of its 62 vills were inhabited by 1086, no doubt as a result of the devastations of 1069-70.

Domesday Book suggests that many of the Anglo-Saxon forms of land tenure survived the Conquest. The main division was between the free and unfree. The freemen (including thegns, drengs and rad-men) had all held their land directly from King Edward, and were differentiated by virtue of special military services peculiar to the frontier regions of England. The unfree (including villeins, bordars, oxmen and slaves) were bound to their masters and to the soil.

In King Edward's time, the highest-ranking freeman had been the thegn. A thegn had important legal privileges and wide judicial powers. Drengs were very similar — landowners and taxpayers with certain duties to perform on the king's land. Radmen (or riding men) ran special errands and performed escort duties for the king. The two largest classes in eleventh-century south Lancashire were the villeins and the bordars. The villein was the common villager who owed his services, not to the king but to the lord of the manor. Although the Domesday Survey does not make clear what these services were, they probably included such duties as castle-guard, carting, cutting timber, tending cattle, shearing sheep and above all, helping with ploughing, mowing and threshing. Villeins had land of their own to cultivate too, perhaps as much as a virgate (about 30 acres (12 ha)), and often they owned plough-oxen. The bordars were cottagers and probably lower on the social scale than the villeins. They may have been freed slaves. In other counties their normal holding was about five acres (2 ha). Oxmen (*bovarii*) were another unfree group who seem, by their name, to have been connected with ploughing.

At the bottom of the social scale came the slaves. Like the oxmen, the slave was principally involved in ploughing and working the lord's land. Some slaves were swineherds or shepherds. In spite of their low status, they seem to have had some rights and even a little property of their own. In their free time they could work for pay and so save up to buy their freedom.

For all these villagers living standards were very primitive. They lived in self-made mud hovels, constructed from pairs of timbers lashed together at the top, anchored in the ground by low, wood-framed walls and roofed with turf or thatch. Inside such a dwelling it was difficult to stand upright, and often the ground was hollowed out to allow extra height. The earthen floor was covered with rushes, straw or furze, cleaned out occasionally when fresh material was available. Animals such as dogs, hens, pigs and cattle — not to mention rats — shared the shelter with members of the family, helping to keep them warm in winter, as did the smoky fire in the middle of the floor. Over this fire the food, mainly porridge and vegetable soups, was cooked. Most households had no facilities for making oatmeal bread or brewing ale, and these were got in from outside. Ewes and cows were both milked, and cheese was an important variant in the diet. Fresh meat was an autumnal treat for some families, when most of the cattle were slaughtered. If salt, brought from Cheshire or Furness, could be afforded, some of the meat was preserved in tubs of brine for consumption through winter. Most households relied on bacon for a little extra flavour. The carcase was hung from a peg in the roof and smoked over the fire. Wool was used for clothes, and hempen cloth was a popular substitute for linen. Life can hardly be considered comfortable when one remembers not only the vulnerability of the coastal plain to flooding and of north Lancashire to Scottish raids, but also the impact on the whole region of cattle sickness, harvest failures and visitations of plague, especially in the Black Death of 1348-9. The only reference to town life in the Lancashire sections of *Domesday Book* concerns Penwortham:

> King Edward held PENEVERDANT (Penwortham). There are two carucates of land and they used to render 10d. Now there is a castle there, and there are two ploughs in the demesne and six burgesses and three radmen and eight villeins and four oxmen. Between them all they have four ploughs. There is a half fishery, woodland, and eyries of hawks, as in the time of King Edward. It is worth 3l.

But six burgesses hardly made a town. They were probably traders who were given special privileges in return for supplying Roger of Poitou's castle. The survey's statistics are not always very reliable, especially for Lancashire, but, to judge by the Penwortham figures, the effect of the Conquest on this one place had been dramatic. The building of the castle had obviously greatly increased the value of the land. Soon, however, Penwortham was to slip back into obscurity when the castle was superseded by Roger's new capital at Lancaster. The monastery which took its place was small and insignificant, and in the twelfth century it was Preston and not Penwortham which received a borough charter.

The Normans built their castles to secure themselves from attack by the native population. The typical early design was the motte and bailey. It simply involved the building of a great mound to support a wooden keep, with an adjacent enclosure or court for keeping animals and for additional out-buildings. The whole was surrounded by a system of ramparts and ditches. The dimensions of the motte varied. At Penwortham the motte was about 30 feet (9 m) high and only 25 feet (7.6 m) in diameter. At Clitheroe, like Penwortham a site which had good natural defences, the motte was 22 feet (6.6 m) above the bailey.

The wooden keeps were one or two-storeyed buildings, occupied by the castle guard, but also intended for the lord's use. Both Penwortham and Warrington began with packed-earth floors covered with rushes and brushwood for warmth and comfort. Later on, when the mounds had settled, the floors and sometimes the keep walls were rebuilt in stone. These replacement stone buildings may still be seen at Lancaster and Clitheroe; in many places only mounds and earthworks remain.

The castles were built for the new upper class which the Norman Conquest imposed on the existing social structure. The new rulers of Lancashire were the followers of Duke William. Count Roger was at their head, but they included other important families like the Lacys of Clitheroe, the Montbegons of Hornby, the de Grelleys of Manchester and the Botelers of Warrington. Such families had far-flung estates and were expected to attend the king. They were therefore rarely in residence. Lancaster Castle, for example, was seldom visited by its owners after being confiscated from Roger of Poitou. King John personally supervised its reconstruction, but this was exceptional. Even the great John of Gaunt, so closely associated with Lancaster by local tradition, is known to have visited the castle which gave him his title only twice in his lifetime, and then just for a few days. Most of his life was spent fighting in France and Spain.

Lancashire's proximity to Wales and Scotland made it an ideal recruiting ground for the campaigns of Edward I. In 1282 William le Boteler, lord of the manor of Warrington, joined the king at Worcester with 200 archers. The archers were well paid — 2d (1p) per day for the ranks and 3d (1½p) for their captains — and William received valuable charters for his growing township near the lowest fording-point of the Mersey (see below). Boteler also joined Edward I on his Scottish campaigns against William Wallace and Robert the Bruce. Periodically throughout the fourteenth and fifteenth centuries help was needed against the Scots and French. When John of Gaunt was Duke of Lancaster military service had to be rendered as far afield as Spain, in pursuit of his claim to the throne of Castile. By then, however, archers were in such demand that they were only being attracted by promises of 6d (2½p) per day.

Post-Conquest society in Lancashire, as elsewhere, was bound together by a hierarchy of social obligations between man and man, from the king at the top to the villein and slave at the bottom, described by historians as feudalism. The king provided protection and justice, land and franchises; in return, the tenants-in-chief (in Lancashire's case, Count Roger) promised their allegiance, which included service at the king's court and military service as required. In war-time they were to provide a certain number of knights. These knights promised loyalty to their lord, as he had done to the king, and in return received maintenance and, later, land. At the bottom of the hierarchy, the villeins and other serfs or bondsmen provided service in the lord's fields and other services in return for land which they could cultivate for their own benefit.

At each level the feudal contract was embodied by the act of homage. A document in mediaeval French in the Lancashire Record Office describes just such an act. It was performed by John Nowell to Thomas of Hesketh at a wapentake court held on Billinge Hill in May 1429. Both parties faced each other bareheaded. Thomas of Hesketh was seated on a great stone, and John Nowell knelt down in front of him, 'face to face' as the clerk recorded. Taking his lord's hands in his own, Nowell said: 'Sir, I will be your man from this day forward, and faith will I bear to you for the lands which I hold of you in Harwood, saving the faith which I owe our lord the king' (Oath of Nowell to Hesketh: Lancashire Record Office). Then Thomas of Hesketh kissed him and held out a holy book, and Nowell put his right hand on it and swore loyalty to him for his freeholding in Harwood, promising to loyally 'perform all the customs and services at the times assigned, so help me God and all the Saints'. Such a scene was commonplace in the Middle Ages.

In the twelfth century knights were granted land for services, or serjeanties, performed at the castle. Land was given for minor tasks as well. Roger de Hesam held two carucates, worth £4 a year, at Heysham for sounding his horn every time the king entered or left the county. William de Parles and William le Gardiner were supposed to supply the castle kitchens in return for land. Ralph de Bolrun took charge of rough masonry work for one carucate worth 20s (£1.00). Ralph de Kellet had to find a carpenter for two oxgangs at Slyne. By the mid-thirteenth century the land was being held by hereditary right, and the service which had formerly justified its possession was frequently commuted to rent. Hence wage labour had to be used to maintain Lancaster Castle.

The barons held their own manor courts and sometimes also acted as the king's justices. Their estates had to be looked after and agents were of limited value. There was a constant stream of petitions

Edmund Crouchback
Earl of Lancaster, 1267-96

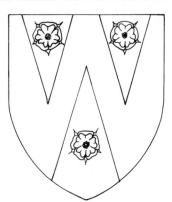

County of Lancaster
granted 1903

John of Gaunt
Duke of Lancaster, 1362-99

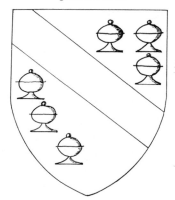

Boteler of Warrington

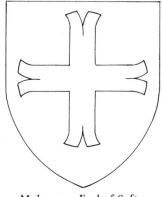

Molyneux, Earl of Sefton

Stanley, Earl of Derby

for favours from tenants, traders demanded markets, and monasteries and churches sought endowment. Possibilities of good hunting also drew the barons to their Lancashire fiefs, especially in winter when they were less likely to be on campaign.

Mediaeval Lancashire was covered by large areas of 'forest' or land set aside for hunting. Much of this land — uncultivated and often, but not always thickly, wooded — had probably been hunted in Anglo-Saxon times. The Norman forest laws were applied, in Count Roger's time, to a large area including Fulwood and Myerscough in Amounderness and Bleasdale, Over Wyresdale, Roeburndale and Quernmore in Lonsdale. In addition, William Rufus gave the de Lacy family, holders of the honour of Clitheroe, rights of free chase and warren over Bowland, Chippingdale, Accrington, Rossendale, Trawden and Pendle and they later added Tottington to these hunting-grounds. All of this Lacy property passed to the honour of Lancaster in 1311 and thus to the crown in 1399. There were other smaller private chases in the county and a coveted gift from the king was such as the 5 bucks and 15 does which Henry II sent from the royal forest of Macclesfield to the Grelley park at Manchester in 1255. In those areas under forest law poachers of deer and wild boars were severely punished by the forest courts, although in 1199 King John had ordered that assarts or clearings made by tenants in the forest should not be interfered with by the royal bailiffs. Such tenants were valuable to the lord in the rents they paid for their vaccaries or dairy farms, where hardy long-haired cattle were bred.

The proportion of land farmed directly by the barons in Lancashire was small. Much of the land was unsuitable and the population too small for the intensive cultivation by serf labour characteristic of the Midlands. The royal estates of Edward the Confessor seem to have been loosely administered and the change of overlordship to Roger of Poitou, on both sides of the Ribble, probably did not bring about major changes in land cultivation. The clearance of woodland, at least in the uplands, was largely carried out by free tenants. Nevertheless, each Lancashire barony had some demesne or home farmland. The manor of Manchester, for example, contained about 1,200 acres of demesne land in 1322, but the ten villeins at Ardwick, Gorton and Crumpsall were paying money rents varying from 4s 5d (22p) to 13s 4d (67p) and were not performing weekly labour services for their lord. Their boon services had not yet been commuted to money payments and still amounted to four days a year, one each for ploughing, harrowing, reaping and carrying corn. Like the free tenants they also had to grind their corn in the lord's mills at Manchester and Gorton, and, unlike the free tenants, were subject to fines at various important moments in his and their lives, such as weddings and funerals.

Monasticism played an important part in the life of mediaeval Lancashire as elsewhere. The first monastery in the region was founded at Lancaster in 1094. Eleven had been founded by 1200, and two more followed in the thirteenth and fourteenth centuries. Only three were ever of any size. These were the house of Augustinian or Austin Canons at Cockersand and the Cistercian abbeys of Furness and Whalley.

The largest Cistercian abbey, Furness, was typical of many Cistercian houses, in that it was established far from the main centres of population in a remote and peaceful country area. Furness, or Bekanesgill as it was originally called, could be approached only from the sea or across the treacherous sands of Morecambe Bay, and so was as suitable as any Cistercian site in Europe. Yet the abbey did not start its life at Furness nor as a Cistercian house. In 1123 Stephen, Count of Mortain, nephew of King Henry I, granted to the monks of Savigny a site for a monastery at Tulketh near Preston. The site was not considered suitable for monks of a reformed order akin to Cîteaux, and four years later they were given a new site in the wilds of Furness. In 1147 Savigny surrendered its independence to Cîteaux, but Furness was the last of its English daughter-houses to submit to this change of allegiance. In spite of a papal bull, Abbot Peter had great difficulty in persuading his monks and he was soon replaced. Nevertheless Furness Abbey remained in practice very independent. It was also a great success. By 1200 the abbey had 'mothered' six daughter houses: one each in Cumberland, Lincolnshire and the Isle of Man and three in Ireland. In terms of land it had acquired about two thousand acres, scattered through North Lonsdale from Walney Island to Ulverston, and beyond into Borrowdale, along the Lune valley, and up to the slopes of Whernside and Ingleborough.

As the Furness estates increased, so did the numbers of monks and lay brothers. There are no figures before 1381, but the buildings suggest perhaps a hundred of each at the peak in the mid-thirteenth century. In the second half of the twelfth century an extensive range of buildings running south from the western end of the abbey nave was provided for the lay brothers, and the church itself was rebuilt. By the mid-thirteenth century a new chapterhouse had been erected, the monks' refectory had been enlarged, and a new dorter, or dormitory, and a warming-house had been put up. The monks' reredorter, or latrine, was extended, and a special infirmary with its own kitchen built. Such was the increase in the abbey's activities that this infirmary was replaced in the early years of the fourteenth century by a huge complex of buildings including an infirmary hall, buttery and chapel. By this time the number of lay brothers as in other Cistercian houses had probably dwindled, and servants with no particular religious calling were taking their place.

We know more about the lives of monks than of many mediaeval people, but little about their home backgrounds. The first monks at Furness were probably French, but later on the richer families of north Lancashire seem to have provided most of the recruits. Most of the abbots had local names, like Walter of Millom (abbot c. 1175), William of Cockerham (abbot in the 1290s) and William of Dalton (abbot c. 1410). While the monks came from the families of the local rich, the lay brothers were probably recruited from the mass of illiterate labourers, and have been aptly described as second-class monks. They swore life-long service to the abbot and were vowed to celibacy. They had the same food as the monks, although they ate and slept separately. They kept silence like the monks and followed a similar, although much shorter, version of the opus Dei, or divine worship, from the abbey nave. They could not read or write, but they were taught the Creed, the Lord's prayer and other simple prayers by heart. Their primary function was to provide unpaid craft labour. With some help from the monks they wove cloth and made habits; they tanned leather and fashioned shoes; they ran the monastery's smithy and carpentry shop; they helped staff the infirmary and took messages; they staffed the granges or outlying farms at places like Beaumont near Lancaster and Winterburn in Yorkshire, and it was they who were the masons who kept the abbey in repair and built the extensions of the late twelfth and early thirteenth centuries.

What kind of day did the monks spend at Furness in the early thirteenth century? Rising about 2.30 am the monks spent the first six hours of their day singing the opus Dei in the choir of the abbey church or praying and reading (by candlelight in winter) huddled up in the cloister. Some orders allowed intervals for the monks to go back to bed, but the Cistercians did not. Mass was celebrated at about 6 am and, after Terce, at about 8.45 am the monks all met together in the chapterhouse. After prayers for the saints of the house, a chapter of St Benedict's Rule was read, and sometimes the abbot preached a sermon. He then issued the orders of the day, and monks who had disobeyed the Rule the previous day confessed and were punished. Punishments varied from bread and water to a whipping, solitary confinement or exile.

After chapter the monks went about their day's work. Some helped the lay brothers. Some copied books in the scriptorium above the chapterhouse, although only one monk, Jocelyn of Furness of the late twelfth century became a writer of any importance. The senior monks helped the abbot to run the monastery and its business. This had become very extensive, in view of the large estates mentioned above. Furness Abbey had 11 granges, none of which by Cistercian rules was more than a day's journey from the house. At the granges such as Beaumont and Winterburn, sheep were reared under the supervision of the lay brothers. How much wool the abbey lands produced is not known, but the abbot's agents probably sold it at the markets of the East Riding and Lincolnshire. Iron was mined and smelted with charcoal on the abbey estates. It became customary for each tenant to receive annually a 'certain clott iron . . . for maintenance of their ploughs and husbandry'. A number of watermills and smithies in the Furness region date from this period. In 1535 the abbey owned five watermills in High Furness alone. Salt was produced at the granges of Salthouse in Furness and Salthus in Copeland. Grain was imported from Ireland. Fish, so important in the monks' diet, reached the abbey from Duddon and the Lune, from Coniston and Windermere. Cattle, reared in the Furness fells, were brought to the fair that the monks licensed six times a year at Dalton, and no doubt the abbot's agents negotiated sales at other fairs too.

Not only was the abbey an important centre of spiritual and economic life; the king looked to the abbot to preserve order and justice on the fringe of the honour of Lancaster. Although a tenant of the king, the abbot of Furness was answerable to no-one else. The orders of the general chapter at Cîteaux and the bulls of the Pope himself had little effect, if opposed by the abbot. Exempt from feudal dues, he had extensive judicial powers, including those of life and death, of which the gibbets at Dalton, Ulverston and Hawkshead acted as grim reminders. After 1344, the abbot of Furness enjoyed the status equivalent to that of sheriff, the king's chief officer in a county.

Although the abbot enjoyed wide powers, his situation presented considerable difficulties. Furness was vulnerable to attack from the sea by pirates such as the bandit-bishop and renegade monk of the abbey, Wimund, who led his Manxmen in raids on abbey property in the 1130s. Wimund was eventually betrayed by some of his own men, and, blinded and mutilated, was sent to end his life, still muttering threats, at Byland Abbey in Yorkshire. The Scots were dealt with less easily. They devastated the abbey estates many times, and, in 1322, King Robert the Bruce added insult to injury by billeting his army in the abbey and its environs. Guests were an important feature in every monastery. At first regarded as a means of spreading the Gospel, they all too easily became a source of income and an excuse for evading the Rule. In remote areas like Furness, travellers were especially dependent on the hospitality of the monks. Even the poorest might expect some charity at the monastery gate and, if sick, a bed in the infirmary. Furness in its later days had a strong tradition of hospitality. The neighbouring houses of Austin Canons at Conishead and Cartmel, apart from the usual charity and hospitality, provided an invaluable additional aid to travellers. Before the turnpike road of 1820 (now the A590) and the Ulverston and Lancaster railway (opened in 1857), the oversands route across Morecambe Bay was the most usual for travellers coming from the south. In the Middle Ages, Cartmel Priory provided a guide for travellers across the Leven, by way of Chapel Island. It is possible, too, that lights were maintained by the monks of Furness at Walney and by those of Cockersand at the mouth of the Lune.

Various social provisions were made by the abbey of Furness for its tenants. The infirmary has already been mentioned, although whether there were any monks at Furness with the medical expertise of Warin of St Albans, trained at Salerno, it is impossible to say. The aim of the infirmary was to obey Christ's words: 'I was sick and you visited me'. Caring for the sick meant adequate food and washing. On medical matters even the independent monks of Furness may have looked to St Bernard, one of the pioneers of the Cistercian Order. He was highly suspicious of doctors and special medicines and for monks in the unhealthy district of the Campagna, near Rome, advised herbal remedies if absolutely necessary: '. . . but to buy special kinds of medicines, seek out doctors and swallow their nostrums, this does not become the religious (monks) . . . the proper medicine is humility . . . ' (from E. Scott-James, *The Letters of St Bernard*, 1953).

Cases of leprosy, which were not uncommon in the twelfth and thirteenth centuries, would have needed special provision. Leper hospitals existed at Lancaster and Preston, and, by the fourteenth century, at Burscough as well. They seem to have enjoyed a certain amount of royal interest and protection. In 1355 the Duke of Lancaster's foreign doctor was made master of the lepers of Preston.

Another service provided by the monks was education. Schools are mentioned at Furness and Upholland in 1535. How early such monastic schools began is hard to say. Although records are patchy it would seem that Lancashire was rather short of secular schools in the Middle Ages, with reference to schoolmasters at only Lancaster and Clitheroe in the late thirteenth century, and Preston in the late fourteenth. In a region where there was a shortage of secular priests, the role of the monks must have been especially important. For the same reason the provision of priests in remote chapels was another important aspect of monastic work. Not counting the benefices in the gift of monasteries, Penwortham, Lytham, Hawkshead, and Ormskirk were all places on or near monastic estates which were supplied with a parish priest by a monastery.

All over Europe in the twelfth century towns were growing and becoming more important. It was one sign of increased population and greater economic activity. Lancashire, although thinly populated, was no exception. *Domesday Book* mentions six burgesses at Penwortham; in the next century there were numerous charters for markets throughout Lancashire. Life was stirring at Colne in 1124 and at Ashton-under-Lyne by 1160. Not all such market towns became boroughs, but many did, and by 1509, there were 20 Lancashire towns with borough charters. The first royal charter to a borough in the county was from Henry II to Preston in 1179. King John chartered Lancaster and Liverpool, and Henry III Wigan. Three boroughs owed their independence to monasteries. Dalton's charter came from Furness, Ormskirk's from Burscough Priory and Kirkham's from the abbot of Vale Royal in Cheshire. Over half of Lancashire's mediaeval boroughs were baronial foundations. Local lords stood to gain as much as anyone from encouraging traders and merchants to settle on their land. Salford's charter was granted by Ranulf, Earl of Chester, Manchester's by Thomas Grelley.

The progress of Warrington is not untypical. The traffic across the Warrington ford was on the increase and so too was the township round the Saxon church and the Norman castle. About 1264 William le Boteler moved out of the castle to a manor house nearby at Bewsey. By 1285 he had got permission from Edward I to hold two weekly markets and two annual fairs. In 1292 he gave his free tenants their first borough charter. They were exempted from payment of tolls at these markets and fairs, given control of the weights and measures used there, and allowed to set up a court independent of the lord of the manor. An additional perquisite was that burgesses were to be allowed free 'pannage' or pasture for their pigs in the lord's woods.

Warrington prospered, like Preston and Lancaster, because it was situated at the lowest fording-point of a major river. In mediaeval times these fords were gradually replaced by bridges. The first mention of a bridge at Warrington was in 1305, sited not far from where the Romans had forded the river. The construction of a bridge did not, however, ensure its continuous upkeep or guarantee it against Mersey floods. Warrington's bridge had to be rebuilt in 1364 and was down again by 1453, when an appeal was made by the bishop for help with its reconstruction. Another bridge was built in 1495 — this time of stone.

A list of tolls in 1310 gives a good idea of the varied nature of Warrington's trade. Local traffic consisted of livestock and such goods as wool, cheese, barley, hides, salt, and fish. Other products came from much further afield, such as cloth from Norfolk, canvas from Galway in Ireland, leather from Spain (as well as Cheshire), and silks, perhaps from France or Italy. Local industry developed on the foundations of this trade. Tanning and brewing became major industries in Warrington in the nineteenth century, but they probably had mediaeval origins. The town grew in the early fourteenth century in the direction of the new bridge. The Austin Friars established a house near the bridge in 1292. The Botelers encouraged the growth by giving their servants burgages or house plots. In 1313 one such grant was to Geoffrey, the lord's cook. Marketgate (now Horsemarket Street) and Newgate (now Bridge Street) began to develop, and the parish church of St Elphin was rebuilt.

The fact that the streets of many mediaeval towns had the suffix '-gate' does not necessarily mean that all towns were protected with high walls and great gatehouses, like mediaeval Chester or York. Warrington and Liverpool had a Marketgate, Manchester a Deansgate, Preston a Friargate and Fishergate, but there is no evidence to suggest that any of these were ever walled towns. Probably there was some kind of ditch to mark the point where borough jurisdiction ended and that of the lord of the manor began. The gates into the town were more like modern customs barriers, with a building where tolls were paid by all strangers bringing in goods to sell in the town. Although the physical extent of Lancashire's mediaeval towns was small, they were not as densely packed with buildings as a modern town centre. The streets might be narrow and the houses over-hanging in places, but behind were gardens belonging to the towns-people and to the monasteries within the town's precincts. In Warrington the friars had their cemetery as well as their garden in the town. The burial-place for the townsfolk was the churchyard round the parish church. Barns and cowhouses were all found where we might expect only houses. Moreover the town straggled, in Warrington's case from the parish church, down modern Church Street, Buttermarket Street and Bridge Street all the way to the bridge. The use of the term 'suburb' in the Legh rental of 1465 indicates the spread of the community by that date.

Many of the houses were single storeyed. Some were semi-detached, described as 'under one roof'. Only the bigger houses had more than one room. In 1465 Lawrence Balfrunte's wife rented from Sir Peter Legh a 'small and fair hall with a high chamber and two shops' in Marketgate, Warrington. Roger Clerk the younger rented a messuage or dwelling in Newgate, 'lately erected with a chamber and solars' (main room and sitting rooms). The description of the house suggests that, like many mediaeval town houses, it had a narrow front and stretched back a good way at right angles to the street. Most houses were of timber construction with walls filled in with wattle and daub. Few survive, although late nineteenth-century rebuilding still gives parts of the town something of the black and white timbered look of the fifteenth century. By 1465 many of the larger houses probably had an aisled hall with a solar or retiring room at one end. Robert Arosmythe rented one such 'principal messuage' with 'solars, kitchen, barn, oven, garden, and appleyard'. The special mention of an oven-house here and there suggests that the less wealthy had to get their bread from a common bakehouse. Although the main fuel was still peat in fifteenth-century Warrington wood and coal were also used. Some houses had a turf or clod house at the back. Tolls levied on coal were first mentioned in the Warrington charter of 1339: a halfpenny a week on every cartload. For water, some houses had private wells, but most relied on communal supplies.

The disposal of rubbish and sewage was a serious problem for mediaeval towns. In the Warrington charter of 1305, William de Hereford was strictly prohibited from placing any dung or filth on the highway or anywhere but on his own land or outside the town. Such conditions were probably disobeyed. Mediaeval towns were notoriously dirty. Attempts were made to pave them from time to time as at Warrington in 1321 and 1338, but with little long-term success. These spasmodic efforts, though ineffectual, show there was some public concern.

Many burgesses held land in the townfields outside the town boundaries. These holdings took the form of strips (lands) or double strips (bilands). By the fifteenth century these were often enclosed by hedges and ditches, replacing the older system of boundary stakes and stones. Developments at Warrington reflect the general tendency towards enclosure in the Lancashire townfields (as the common fields were usually called) from the thirteenth and four-teenth centuries onward. By the fifteenth century a mixture of rents and services were owed by farmers and townspeople alike, although the services in the Legh rental of 1465 rarely amounted to more than a couple of days in the autumn, and, as elsewhere, were generally commuted to cash. The busy burgesses would no doubt have been as keen as the local farmer to pay the 4d (2p) value of two days' service at harvest-time, rather than provide the labour themselves. They still had to grind their corn at the lord's mill, but, at Warrington, there was a choice of three.

5 TUDOR AND EARLY STUART TIMES

Lancashire was a county of paradoxes in the early sixteenth century. The duchy of Lancaster had given its name to one of the two houses contesting the throne in the fifteenth century, yet the Wars of the Roses had hardly touched the north-west. No major battle was fought in Lancashire, even though it occupied a strategic place in the disposition of crown lands. Henry VI had taken refuge in the north-west after his defeat at Hexham in 1464, and had been betrayed at Bolton-by-Bowland, but otherwise the wars did not extend to Lancashire, even though many Lancastrians fought in the royal army. When the Yorkists consolidated their position as the ruling house in the 1470s, Lancashire nobles were expected to provide troops for the King in spite of the recent civil war. The forces of Lord Thomas Stanley were eagerly awaited by Richard III at the battle of Bosworth in 1485, but Stanley's defection to Henry, Earl of Richmond, proved Richard's downfall. Henry Tudor, once crowned Henry VII, gave Stanley his reward — elevation to the earldom of Derby and marriage to Henry Tudor's mother, the Lady Margaret Beaufort.

Lancashire at this time was a poor region, a fact borne out by tax returns from the fourteenth to the seventeenth centuries and emphasised by the small number of castles and monasteries. The considerable extent of Lancashire parishes provided an adequate income for their incumbents, but the beneficed clergy were often non-resident and their curates were poorly paid. Lancashire churches had few resources lavished on them and there was a shortage of spare money even for vestments. The county's population, however, more than doubled between the late fourteenth and the mid-sixteenth centuries. Dr C. Haigh estimates it as about 95,000 in 1563.

The first half of the sixteenth century was marked by the growth of domestic cloth manufacture, with centres at Bolton, Rochdale and, above all Manchester. Population pressure led to the gradual clearance of former forests, such as Bowland, and the division and enclosure of common arable fields and pastures. Lancashire was still primarily a cattle county, but the demands of the woollen industry led to some increase in sheep-farming, especially in east Lancashire. Many Lancastrians left the county to obtain preferment or wealth elsewhere, but many also used their new-found prosperity to endow chantries, chapels and schools in their native towns or villages.

There is every sign of strong Catholic piety in pre-Reformation Lancashire. This showed itself, in 1537, in the enthusiasm for the Pilgrimage of Grace, a demonstration against Henry VIII's dissolution of the monasteries. This piety was not easily diverted by the Reformation and took new life in lay recusancy and in provision and protection of Roman Catholic priests under Elizabeth. Spiritual determination also showed itself in highly active Puritanism. Legal records, however, show that these were also violent times. Although the Earl of Derby maintained overall control as the king's lord lieutenant, he had to be very vigilant to prevent the gentry from coming to blows. As late as 1617, by which time James I had even pacified the Scottish borders, Nicholas Assheton of Downham had to go to the rescue of his aunt in Wensleydale, where she was besieged by Sir Thomas Metcalfe with 40 armed men. Assheton did not risk a fight, but he stayed long enough to see justice done. Three days after the initial outrage, Sir Thomas was arrested by officials from the Council of the North at York. Six of his men were arrested with him, and the rest dispersed.

Until 1541 the ecclesiastical administration of the county was divided between York and Lichfield, while the archdeacon of Richmond had wide powers, semi-independent of the archbishop of York. After 1541 Lancashire's spiritual life was governed from Chester, but the bishops there did not find the going easy. In matters of spiritual concern they found powerful critics in the Puritan preachers of east Lancashire and the recusant Roman Catholic priests in the aftermath of the Reformation.

Life became generally more comfortable for the Lancashire gentry in the sixteenth century. Many new houses were built. Sir

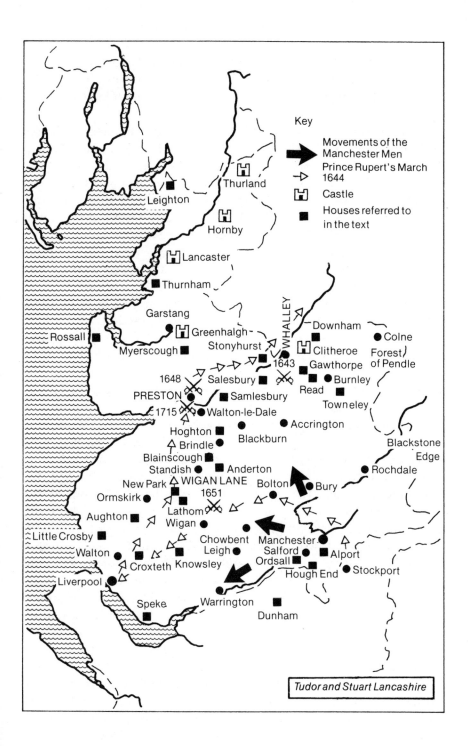

Key

Movements of the Manchester Men

Prince Rupert's March 1644

⌂ Castle

■ Houses referred to in the text

Thurland

Leighton

Hornby

⌂ Lancaster

Thurnham

Garstang

⌂ Greenhalgh

Rossall

Myerscough

Stonyhurst

WHALLEY

Downham

Colne

Clitheroe

Forest of Pendle

1643

Gawthorpe

1648

Salesbury

Burnley

Read

PRESTON

Samlesbury

Towneley

1715

Walton-le-Dale

Hoghton

Accrington

Brindle

Blackburn

Blainscough

Blackstone Edge

Standish

Anderton

Rochdale

New Park

WIGAN LANE

Bolton

Ormskirk

1651

Bury

Lathom

Aughton

Wigan

Little Crosby

Chowbent

Manchester

Walton

Leigh

Salford

Alport

Croxteth

Knowsley

Ordsall

Stockport

Liverpool

Hough End

Speke

Warrington

Dunham

Tudor and Stuart Lancashire

Richard Molyneux built Croxteth Hall about 1575. Many more, like Stonyhurst and Hoghton Tower, were rebuilt. Some, like Speke and Rufford, received considerable modernisation and additions.

Some of the changes are reflected in the development of Speke Hall, near Liverpool. The present hall was begun by Sir William Norris about 1490, and took the form of a great hall, with a dais at one end for the owner and his family and an open fire in the centre of the room. The hall had a solar at one end where the lord would find privacy after dinner. His servants would sleep round the fire in the hall. This arrangement at Speke *circa* 1500 was the standard late mediaeval arrangement. Changes were made by Sir William's grandson, also called William, who succeeded to the house in 1524. He divided the great hall with a double partition or screen, so making a passage across the hall from the courtyard to the garden. At the same time he put a fireplace in what was left of the hall, and built on the great parlour to replace the solar. At the same time he had both rooms panelled, and put a ceiling in the hall to make it less draughty. Additional buildings occupied three sides of the courtyard. Further improvements were made by his successors throughout the sixteenth century.

An inventory, dated 1624, gives a good impression of the increase in comfort that a Lancashire gentleman of modest means could expect by the beginning of the seventeenth century. By 1624 there were two parlours and a withdrawing room as well as the hall, for entertaining guests. The great parlour was the chief room of the house, with 'the king's arms cut in wood, hanging on the wall', a long table covered with a green carpet, three chairs 'covered with green and fringed with green silk' and two little chairs covered similarly. To sit in a chair was still a great privilege, accorded only to the elderly, the sick or the most important guests. For the majority of the family and their visitors there were 24 upholstered stools, and six cushions of Arras work. Green curtains hung in the windows. In the little parlour there was another long table and more stools. There were also three pairs of tables for cards or chess. On the wall was a map of Jerusalem.

The chief persons of the household had their own rooms. 'My Lord's' was the grandest. Its main feature was 'one standing bed with curtain rods, the tester of branched damask green and yellow, with a deep silk fringe of the same colour'. On the bed were a feather bed and a down bed, a bolster, two pillows, four blankets (three of which were Spanish), and a green silk quilt covering. Other furniture included a chair, two stools and a cupboard, and there was a window seat, with two cushions, made from cloth of silver and gold. The room was also equipped with firearms and chamber-pots. For the children there were two nurseries and a school chamber. The Norrises were Roman Catholics and a special room was set aside as a chapel.

Around the hall were the fields and woods which gave Speke its wealth. In 1624 the Norrises added up their livestock and farm implements as well as their cushions and curtains. The home farm had a dairy herd of 23 'milch kine' and five 'northern beasts' for fattening. There were 44 sheep — mainly fat wethers — and a dozen oxen for pulling carts, ploughs and harrows. The number of ordinary folk who would have wielded the spades and pitchforks was not mentioned.

The Norrises were one of the leading Lancashire families, but the most important man in the county was the Earl of Derby. As lord lieutenant, he was the monarch's representative in the north-west. Elizabeth sent her orders to him and he carried them out as far as he could, through his own council and the justices of the peace. The earl lived like a king — indeed as Lord of Man he was virtually a king in his own right. In 1587, on the eve of the Armada, Henry Stanley, the fourth earl, had a household of 118 people when he returned from court to set up house at Lathom near Ormskirk. When he sat down to eat in the great hall there, he was attended by a page and seven young gentlemen waiters, all drawn from the chief families of the county. They were learning to take a lead in local society from the greatest man in the county. Three of the earl's gentlemen had been abroad with him on embassies to France and the Netherlands. Such posts were a means of entering the royal service.

Lord Derby's 'court' attracted a large number of different types of people. There were occasional visits from royalty, although Elizabeth did not travel so far from London. Various nobles came to stay at Knowsley, like the Queen's favourite, Lord Dudley. On one occasion, the Earl of Tyrone, the most powerful man in Ireland, stayed with the Stanleys on his way south to see the Queen. There was a constant flow of less exalted visitors; the local gentry, both Catholic and Protestant came, curious for news of the court and anxious for favours. The Bishop of Chester came to discuss the handling of recusants and Puritans; the Mayor of Liverpool came to ensure good relations between his borough and the leading local landowner. Tenants came to discuss estate business, to pay their rents and to negotiate new leases. The poor came to the gatehouse for a share of the surplus food distributed from the kitchens.

The earl passed on instructions from the government and asked his friends for advice. He could then inform the Queen's ministers of the state of opinion in his part of the Kingdom. His news was eagerly sifted at court, for Lancashire's loyalty was of vital importance at a time when there were internal troubles as well as threats from Ireland, Scotland and Spain. The news from Lancashire must usually have reassured Elizabeth and her government.

Many local gentlemen were Roman Catholic, but they were not looking for trouble. By political loyalty they hoped to escape the worst of the penalties for recusancy or refusal to attend reformed church services. A fine of one shilling (5p) was levied on non-attenders, but repeated absence often led to imprisonment.

The earl was often away. He had his estates to supervise and there were the quarter sessions at Ormskirk, Preston, or Lancaster to attend. In any spare time, he went hunting, at Alport near Manchester, Lathom or Knowsley. The venison was eaten at table afterwards.

Although the earl moved around a great deal, his household did not always move with him, but tended to rotate between his four Lancashire residences of Lathom, and neighbouring New Park, Knowsley and Alport. It was a major event when the household moved. Furniture and furnishings all had to be moved too, for, in spite of his wealth, the earl did not keep all his houses furnished all the year round. This is hardly surprising when simply feeding the household cost £1,500 a year.

Nine men were employed in the kitchen, but no women — indeed the only women on the 'chekeroll' were the two laundresses. Only the master-cooks were allowed to dress his lordship's meat, and all those not employed in the kitchen were banned from it at such times for fear of poisoners. The household had its own bakehouse and brewery. The servants ate a special 'household bread', composed of equal parts of wheat and barley, and drank a special beer made from oat malt. There was a slaughter house too. Fish for Lent was purchased at Stourbridge Fair, near Cambridge, but for the rest of the year the Derby estate was self-sufficient for its main needs.

Meals at the Stanley table were both large and varied. William ffarington described the ordinary weekly consumption of the household as 'about one ox, a dozen calves, a score of sheep, fifteen hogs-heads of ale, and plenty of bread, fish and poultry'. The earl sat at the high table with his wife and family, and everyone was served in strict order of rank. The high table was served by gentlemen waiters.

Henry Stanley, the fourth earl, was entertained by his fool also called Henry. There may have been musicians too, although none except the trumpeters are mentioned in the roll. Lord Strange — the earl's eldest son and deputy when he was away — had his own company of players. They did not perform exclusively at Lathom or Knowsley. In 1581 they provided the Queen's New Year's enter-tainment at Court, by 'sundry feats of tumbling and activity'. On other occasions they performed short plays. Every few months a company of visiting players came to entertain the earl. The most regular visitors at the time of the Armada were the Queen's Players. It is possible that William Shakespeare appeared before Lord Derby with one of these companies. On Sundays and special days the earl heard sermons in chapel from his chaplain.

The standard of living of the Earl of Derby and the gentry was in marked contrast with that of the vast majority of Lancastrians in the sixteenth century. While the gentry lived in their newly extended manor-houses, the cottages of the people remained as they had been for centuries. Most still lived in dwellings erected on the cruck sys-tem, with a pair of oak timbers set up at either end and secured by collar and tie beams. The walls were still made of wattle and daub, and the roofs were still thatched, with a hole to let out the smoke. Yet changes were on the way, at least in the homes of yeomen and farmers. Extra rooms were being pushed out at either end of the dwelling to provide separate or additional cooking and sleeping accommodation. Upper floors were being added, too, which meant the need for fireplaces and chimneys. Screens, passages, porches, built-in cupboards and long mullioned windows were introduced in farmhouses in the sixteenth and seventeenth centuries. Brick and stone were much more frequently used. Stone slabs or 'Lancashire slates' were even beginning to replace thatch. Yeomen's homes were now more spacious, healthier, more durable and being of brick or stone less susceptible to fire. Labourers' cottages were eventually influenced by these changes, too. By the eighteenth century the wood and mud cabins of earlier days were being replaced by two-roomed stone cottages, particularly in the upland areas where building stone was most accessible.

During the sixteenth century the gradual rearrangement of many of the townfields into compact blocks accelerated. This process of voluntary enclosure had begun as early as the thirteenth century in Lancashire. One suggested reason for this is that many common fields were small and only shared by a few farmers. Some common cultivation of arable townfields however, survived on the Lancashire plain. Hence in 1612, 'all and every freeholders and occupiers of the Townfields' in Leyland were instructed to 'remove and take all their cattle out of the said Townfields yearly at or before the feast day of the Annuncon (Annunciation) of the blessed virgin Mary, commonly called Lady Day in Lent (25 March)', according to ancient custom and in time for the spring sowing. Large amounts of moorland and peatmoss remained unenclosed, for the use of all, until the eighteenth and nineteenth centuries, although there was a good deal of reclamation of marginal land by individual free-holders.

Holdings were small — rarely over 30 acres. The small farmers and yeomen lived off their animals, mainly cows and a few sheep, and, where the land was suitable, they planted oats. In south-west Lancashire more wheat was grown. Little is known of the systems of crop rotation. The use of 'outfields' to give the 'infields' a rest after a number of years of intensive cultivation may have been common.

Domestic cloth-making was an important subsidiary industry. The principal raw materials were flax from west Lancashire, and later Ireland, and wool from the Pennines. These were bought from dealers or chapmen, if not available locally. At Hoole the Shuttleworths grew flax and their tenants spun it into yarn. Wives and children usually did the spinning, while husbands wove the yarn into cloth on the loom. With the growth of the yarn trade in the sixteenth century, the farmer-weaver came to rely on yarn put out to him by a clothier from one of the towns. The cloth would be made up for a certain day of the week, and either collected by the chapman or taken into the clothier's warehouse by one of the family. In the course of the eighteenth century the domestic system became more specialized, and a great variety of goods was produced. Some weavers came to concentrate wholly on their weaving and acquired loom-shops where they employed others, but for the most part this domestic system survived with little basic alteration until the hand-loom was replaced by the power-loom in the course of the nineteenth century.

Although the cloth trade had a variety of local centres, the regional capital of both the linen and woollen industries was Manchester. It is difficult to ascertain if the skills of weaving and finishing cloth had been taught to Mancunians by foreign immigrants. What is certain is that Manchester could only benefit from the arrival of victims of religious persecution in the Netherlands and elsewhere in the sixteenth century. The importance of Manchester as a cloth market was acknowledged in 1565 when Parliament appointed 'aulnagers' to stamp woollen cloth once it was ready for sale. This assured minimum quality and measurements in each piece of cloth. Only a year later Manchester's governing body, the Court Leet, was issuing a standard version of weights and measures to ensure uniformity of products. Linens, such as 'Preston cloth' and 'Stockport cloth', were mainly for the home market, but, by Elizabeth's reign, Lancashire woollens were being exported, with Rouen as the chief continental market.

The number of Manchester merchants who dealt directly with continental buyers was small, but there was a growing group of cloth merchants whose wealth could rival that of the local gentry. Their activities extended from 'putting out' yarn to country weavers and 'taking in' the cloth for bleaching and finishing, to sending off consignments of cloth and smallwares (such as tapes and ticking) by packhorse to the great fairs of Stourbridge, near Cambridge, or St Bartholomew in London. James Chetham, who died in 1571, sold his wares to agents at the ports of Hull, Liverpool and Chester. From the early seventeenth century such exports included fustian, an increasingly popular type of cloth made from a mixture of Irish flax and 'cotton wool' (raw cotton) imported from the Levant.

The clothiers were not as rich or powerful in Manchester as in the West Country, and most of them lived in quite modest town houses. Yet their wills indicate that they often owned considerable personal possessions as well as land and cottage property both let for rent. When Isabel Holland, the widow of a Salford merchant, died in 1598 she left pieces of silver plate and a silver pot, and, to her son Richard, she bequeathed her 'best standing bed', with a feather mattress and a whole set of bedding. Her home was evidently furnished as well as Speke Hall. Some Manchester merchants, like Nicholas Mosley, were becoming men of more than local importance.

Looking after the London end of his family business he became alderman and Lord Mayor of London in 1599. In 1596 he bought the manor of Manchester for £3,500 from a London mercer, John Lacy and built Hough End Hall at Chorlton-cum-Hardy.

Manchester was a small but growing town in Tudor times with a population, along with neighbouring Salford, of only a few thousands. Many of the tradesmen and weavers still had land outside the town as well as a shop in Cateaton Street or Smithy Door. Dr Dee, warden of the Collegiate Church at the end of Elizabeth's reign, was sent 17 cattle by his Welsh relations to graze on the college fields. Those engaged in textiles used the surrounding fields as 'tenters' or bleaching grounds at certain times in the year. An Act of Parliament of 1540 referred to this practice, and travellers passing through east Lancashire in the seventeenth and eighteenth centuries were still remarking that the fields were white with cloth slowly bleaching in the sun.

The town was governed by the Court Leet which met twice a year and which 'all and every the inhabitants and householders of the town of Manchester' were summoned to attend. In fact few of them did so, and decisions were made by the dozen or so jurors who were chosen by the steward from the leading local families. The court belonged to the lord of the manor, but the lords de la Warre who held the manor until 1579 were usually absentees in the south of England, having given their manor house in Manchester as a home for the college of priests in 1423. In the 1560s their steward was the Earl of Derby who sometimes presided, but more often left the chair to a deputy, usually a lawyer. With the help of the jurors, disputes between local people were settled, and, with the help of its officials, the court supervised the sale of goods, regulated weights and measures, and tried to enforce certain standards of public hygiene and behaviour. In 1573 John Skilliescorn, a plumber, was brought before the court as a common 'easing dropper (eavesdropper), a naughty person, such a one as doth abound in all mysorders'. He was to be 'avoided the Town and have such punishment as unto such doth appertain'.

Hygiene was primitive. Manchester relied for its fresh water supply on a wooden conduit leading from a spring in Spring Gardens to the market place. The Court Leet tried to protect its use. It appointed two men to keep the market place clean and tried to make the neighbouring householders responsible for its upkeep. In 1579 the

1 Prehistoric weapons and tools:
1   Axe-hammer from Rawtenstall
2   Flint javelin head
3 & 4   Celt and palstave (chisels)
5   Arrow-heads
6   Barbed arrow-heads
7   Neolithic axe-head from Manchester
8   Sickle flint (above) and scraper

2 Manchester cryptogram. A Christian cryptogram concealing the words *Pater Noster* with A (Alpha) and O (Omega), found in a late second-century rubbish pit in the settlement attached to the fort

3 *Left* Ribchester Fort. An imaginary reconstruction of Roman Ribchester in the late second century A.D., from the south-west. Note the parade ground and *vicus*. The river Ribble has since changed its course

4 Ribchester ceremonial parade helmet and mask. Made of bronze, and dating from the late first century A.D., it was found in the river bank in 1796 and is now in the British Museum

5 Silver Penny of Athelstan (925-40 AD). Even if his title, REX TOTIUS BRITANNIAE, was an exaggerated boast, his victories over the Danes, Norsemen and Scots brought much of the future Lancashire under Wessex's control

6 Whalley churchyard cross. The later of two stone crosses at Whalley dates from the eleventh century and represents the Tree of Calvary. Parts of the head and shaft are missing

7 Lancaster castle gatehouse. This gatehouse was rebuilt by Henry IV (1399-1413), first king of the House of Lancaster. The statue (1822) is of his father, John of Gaunt. The cottages were demolished in 1876

8 The Bull's Head, Greengate, Salford. This mediaeval timbered inn — now demolished — with its cellars hewn out of solid rock, once incorporated the cottage of cruck design on the left

9 Seal of Thomas, 2nd Earl of Lancaster, 1301. The leader of the baronial opposition to Edward II and Gaveston, he was executed for treason after his defeat at Boroughbridge in 1322. (British library reference: Howe. ch. 43 c. 46 seal)

10 Furness Abbey, from the south-west. From their arrival in 1127 until their dispersal in 1537, the monks of Furness controlled large estates north and east of Morecambe Bay

11 The courtyard, Speke Hall, near Liverpool. Begun *c.* 1490, it shows such typical contemporary features as herringbone bracing, quatrefoils, wooden pegging and lattice windows. The roof is made of Lancashire stone 'slates'

12 Pendle Hill. Pendle was formerly a royal forest, but cattle were replacing deer by 1612 when 19 local people were tried at Lancaster in the most famous witch trial in English history

13 Old Lathom House. This is a romanticised reconstruction of the former chief seat of the Stanleys, of which only the chapel survived destruction after the sieges of 1644 and 1645

14 Execution of James, Earl of Derby, at Bolton, 1651, as shown in a reconstruction of 1785. After the battle of Worcester, the Earl was brought to the town which he and Prince Rupert had sacked in 1644

court restricted the use of the water, by having the conduit covered and locked between 9 pm and 6 am and by insisting that the women who carried the water should queue up in turn and only fetch as much water as they could carry. In 1585 housewives were ordered not to do their washing or their washing up in the conduit or to wash the 'meats of beasts' there. No doubt they did so when the market officials were not looking, or went down to the river instead. The rivers Irk and Irwell had all manner of rubbish tipped into them, including carrion.

Such conditions encouraged the spread of disease. 'Sickness' or plague was a constant visitor to Elizabethan Manchester. The 1581 outbreak was the natural consequence of the poor harvest of 1580. Again in 1586, a bad harvest brought serious shortage, bread doubled in price and the 'sickness' followed. Plague struck again in 1590, and 70 people died in April alone. So bad was the outbreak of 1604-5 that six acres of wasteland at Collyhurst, outside the town, had to be set aside for the wooden cabins of the plague sufferers and the pits where 2,000 victims were buried. In better years the townspeople kept their geese and pigs at Collyhurst, although so many also kept pigs at home that in 1567 the Court Leet appointed a swineherd to drive them out of town in the morning and bring them back at night. Archery contests had also been held there but, by the late sixteenth century, archery had been largely superseded by football as the favourite sport of the apprentices.

Manchester's growth had been acknowledged by the founding of the magnificent Collegiate Church by Thomas de la Warre in 1421 and by the endowment of a free school by the Manchester-born Bishop of Exeter, Hugh Oldham, in 1515. The influence of the Renaissance spirit may be seen in Oldham's statutes, for although he paid tribute to the 'pregnant wit' of his fellow Mancunians, he noted with regret that they were 'mostly brought up rudely and idly and not in virtue or cunning or good manners'. The school was designed to correct this and to ensure that the children grew up to 'know, love, honour and dread God and his laws'. The foundation was sited between the college and the river Irk, and was well endowed with the rents from various properties and the profits of the town's corn mills.

From Oldham's statutes it is possible to reconstruct the kind of day that a boy would have spent at the free school in the sixteenth century. Arriving at 7 am in winter, or an hour earlier in the summer, unless a late boy for some reason, he would begin the day with the others by saying the *Deus miseratur*. Then the scholars would separate: the infants to one end of the long room known as 'the school' to be taught their *ABC* from a primer by one of the senior scholars: the seniors to the other end where they were taught by the master. The juniors were taught in another room by the deputy master or usher. On Wednesdays and Fridays there was a procession in church in which the scholars took part, reciting the common litany and the *De Profundis* for the souls of Hugh Oldham and other benefactors. This practice was altered at the Reformation, when annual commemoration of benefactors replaced bi-weekly intercession. On other days the boys would be in school all day until about 5 pm with one break in their studies for dinner. This meal was provided by the school for those who could afford it; the rest took their own food to an eating-house in the town. The break at midday was not a time for total relaxation, for Bishop Oldham insisted that Latin should be spoken at all times on the school premises. The end of the day was marked by assembly for the *Magnificat* and the *De Profundis* about 5 pm.

On special days, if the warden of the college gave his permission, 'honest games' could be played. These were not specified, but presumably included all games without any element of gambling or violence. Cock-fighting, so popular in many schools on Shrove Tuesday, when the master was traditionally bribed with 'cock-pennies', was specifically prohibited at Manchester. Offensive weapons were banned as well, although boys eating dinner in school were expected to bring their own meat-knives. Boys who caused an 'affray' were automatically suspended for a month. On the third offence the offender was expelled. Oldham made no mention of corporal punishment, but it was no doubt used as frequently as in other schools of the period.

If games were not part of the curriculum, they were certainly enjoyed after school hours. Football was a common sport of the time. So too also to the dismay of the Court Leet, was a game called giddy-gaddy or tipcat. Like a primitive sort of cricket, it involved flicking a ball or piece of wood tapered at both ends, off the ground and knocking it as far as possible. The Court Leet tried to restrict the game to children. Any player over twelve (later seven) years old was liable to a fine or, for a short spell, 'to be imprisoned in the dungeon' (built out of the ruins of an old chapel on Salford bridge).

Apart from holy days allowed by the warden, the only days on which the pupils did not have to attend the school were four days at both Christmas and Easter. The master and usher each had 20 days off a year, but they were not to be away at the same time. Probably the school was closed quite often by plague, and individual boys were not admitted if they were suffering from any 'horrible or contagious infirmity infective, such as pox, leprosy, pestilence for the time being'.

The Reformation brought alterations in the church services and new manuals for use in schools. Latin, however, remained the language of scholars, and its teaching continued to preoccupy grammar school boys, if only because without it they would not be eligible for scholarships at the universities. In Manchester's case there were closed scholarships at Brasenose College, Oxford. University now provided a gateway to careers in medicine and law as well as the Church. Grammar schools sprang up in the wake of Bishop Oldham's foundation all over the county. Some were in towns, like Warrington (1520), Kirkham (1551), Clitheroe (1554) and Bury (1625). Others were set up in rural areas, such as Penwortham (later Hutton) (1552) and Warton (1594). Most of these schools were conducted in the church or in buildings, like Manchester's, erected close by. Most of the country schools concentrated on reading and writing. Town grammar schools, like Manchester or Lancaster, sent a steady stream of pupils to the universities; country ones, like Penwortham or Warton, sent hardly any.

The north-west was in the front line of religious controversy in the late sixteenth century. The county had resisted the dissolution of the monasteries and it opposed the middle path between Protestantism and Roman Catholicism which Elizabeth chose as her ecclesiastical policy. Many of the gentry clung on to the old faith and refused to attend the new church services. The Pope excommunicated Elizabeth, and devout Roman Catholics found their loyalties divided between pope and crown. From 1580 Jesuit and secular priests, trained at Rome and Douai, began their missionary activities to strengthen the recusants and to regain lost ground. Lancashire was one of their most important targets.

The most famous of the Jesuits was Edmund Campion. After a brilliant career at Oxford and various universities on the continent, he joined the party of 14 priests who landed in England in the spring of 1580. After a few months in London and the Welsh borders, he moved into Lancashire in January 1581, travelling from one recusant's house to another, celebrating Mass and preaching to large gatherings of neighbours. His itinerary is by no means certain, but, among other places, he stayed at Blainscough with the Worthingtons, Salesbury with the Talbots, Samlesbury with the Southworths, Aughton with the Heskeths, and Rossall with the sister-in-law of William Allen, the founder of the English colleges at Dovai and Rome, and who became a Cardinal in 1587. Government agents were searching for Campion, and he had to make use of what hiding-places his hosts could provide. On one occasion he narrowly escaped arrest by being pushed into a pond by a servant.

Edmund Campion was caught soon after he left Lancashire. He was taken to the Tower of London, tortured on the rack, tried at Westminster Hall, and executed at Tyburn on 1 December 1581. To Elizabeth's government he and his fellow Jesuits were 'a sort of hypocrites . . . a rabble of vagrant friars, whose principal errand was to creep into the houses of men of behaviour and reputation, to corrupt the realm with false doctrine, and, under that pretence, to stir up rebellion'. Yet Campion's mission was not political. He was remembered in Lancashire for his ministry to the Roman Catholic faithful and was canonized in 1970.

Other priests and Roman Catholic laity suffered too. In 1581, by Act of Parliament, the fine for saying Mass was increased to 200 marks (£133.33) and one year's imprisonment, and the penalty for hearing it was almost as steep. The fine for non-attendance at the parish church on Sundays and holy days was put up to £20 monthly per person. Schoolmasters, who were often priests in disguise, were to be fined £10 a month for non-attendance, forbidden to teach and imprisoned for a year. Under the terms of this Act Dr Chadderton, Bishop of Chester, was instructed to root out the recusants and priests in his diocese. In January 1584 a list was made of 38 Roman Catholics who had been tried at Manchester and committed to Salford gaol. They included 12 priests, 3 schoolmasters, various gentlemen, and a few yeomen and craftsmen. A special imposition was laid on the Convocations of York and Canterbury for their upkeep. Elsewhere in the county committals were more difficult to obtain. Recusants frequently received rough treatment from those searching for them. Some fled, others were put in prison. Sir John Southworth, a former sheriff of the county, and John Towneley, brother-in-law of the Protestant Alexander Nowell,

Dean of St Paul's, were kept in the New Fleet Prison at Salford. Lady Southworth, as one of Burghley's informers reported, was not deterred by her husband's fate: 'At the lodge in Samlesbury Park there be Masses daily, and seminaries (priests) divers resort thither, as James Coupe, Harrison, Bell and such like'. This was the most advanced form of recusancy. Yet there were even wives and families of supposedly Protestant magistrates who did not attend church and were either known or suspected papists.

While Roman Catholicism was strengthened by the like of Edmund Campion and the Southworths, the reformed religion began to make progress in south-east Lancashire. The important cloth centre of Manchester, fed by the surrounding villages and towns, and sending goods to London and abroad, became the capital of Lancashire Puritanism, from where literature and ideas could spread along established trade routes. The propagandists were the Puritan clergy who had attended those colleges at Oxford and Cambridge most influenced by Protestant theology. Having proceeded to university from the new grammar schools, these young men returned to Lancashire with the same enthusiasm as their Jesuit opponents, anxious not only to engage in the war against ungodliness and popery, but also to win over the local laity.

Puritanism was characterized partly by an emphasis on the sermon as the teaching part of the service, partly by the attack on all remaining 'rags of Rome' such as the surplice and the sign of the cross at baptism. To show their liberation from popish 'superstition', Puritans regarded it as unnecessary to kneel at Communion or to remove hats in church. Religious zeal was not confined to church. Puritans held meetings for prayer and bible study, and attached great importance to family devotions. The Puritan household, like its Roman Catholic counterpart, had to be a model of the godly community. Such households welcomed Puritan preachers as enthusiastically as Roman Catholic households welcomed the missionary priests.

Puritanism established its bases in the parish churches of east Lancashire and gradually fanned out from there. From the 1580s schemes to provide extra preachers and ministers to serve in the vast Lancashire parishes were financed by the Puritan laity. Even Elizabeth, who bitterly resisted the Puritans where they challenged the god-given authority of herself and her bishops, found no alternative but to extend the sphere of puritan preaching in 1599 by endowing

77

four Queen's preachers with salaries of £50 a year, to supplement the work of the parish clergy in a county where the established Church had insufficient resources for its task. The main contribution, however, was from the leading laymen. More churches were desperately needed. Some were provided in rural areas where there was no previous building, such as Much Hoole, near Preston, endowed in 1629 by Thomas Stones, a London haberdasher. Others were provided in growing towns, such as the chapel at Salford, established in 1634, by Humphrey Booth, a local gentleman clothier. By the reign of Charles I the puritans had established themselves as the most powerful and vigorous element in the Church in Lancashire.

While Roman Catholic priests and Puritan preachers campaigned to bring their versions of the Gospel to the people, popular religion remained a mixture of magic and superstition. Largely unprotected from the ever-present threat of sickness to humans and animals alike, and with insufficient medical knowledge to provide a basis for informed remedies, men and women looked to charms for protection. Most villages probably had charmers, wise men or women, who were regarded as having special powers of divination and prediction and who could command life, death and disease. Their remedies might consist of a charm or a herbal potion. The powers of wizards were regarded as a gift and were often viewed as hereditary. Henry Baggilie, examined at Chadderton near Oldham in 1634, confessed to the Lancashire magistrates that he always used a charm which his father had been taught by a Dutchman.

It was believed that such powers could be used for both good and evil. The sudden death of adults, children and animals alike was the experience of every family. Medical symptoms were sometimes recognized, but there was no-one to diagnose them. Although the divine will was an explanation for the educated, evil spirits, fairies or witchcraft seemed more satisfactory to the majority. Sometimes, the blame might be placed on some unpopular section of society such as the Roman Catholics. For example, William Brettergh, a Protestant who lived near Liverpool, in an area largely inhabited by Roman Catholics, unquestioningly attributed the death of his horse and cattle by night to 'seminary priests and recusants that lurked thereabouts'.

Witchcraft was a popular explanation for misfortune. It was encouraged by the revival of academic interest in magic and astrology in sixteenth-century England. The magicians denied a separation between natural and supernatural phenomena and believed that everything was explicable in terms of a universal soul. The age-old interest in astrology was now supplemented by the magical belief that man could divert astral influences by the use of talismans and spells. Although such beliefs were regarded with suspicion by the Church they were often held side by side with an orthodox Christian faith. Perhaps the most famous English astrologer was Dr John Dee, the friend and protégé of Queen Elizabeth, whom she made Warden of Manchester Collegiate Church in 1595. All kinds of stories were told about his dealings with spirits, including one that with his assistant, a man called Kelly, he had evoked the spirit of a dead person in the churchyard at Walton-le-Dale. Magicians were frequently misrepresented, and there is probably little truth in many of these stories about Dr Dee.

Puritan teachers were active in condemning both magic and witchcraft. They saw the world of the spirit divided between the embattled powers of Christ and Anti-Christ (or the Devil), just as the material world was divided between Protestants and Roman Catholics. In this battle between good and evil, militant Protestants associated their opponents not simply with error, but frequently with active Devil-worship. Like James I, Puritan ministers in east Lancashire identified witchcraft along with the Roman Catholic Church as the work of the Devil and indeed these Puritan ministers were so active in the work of 'dispossession' or exorcism of troubled spirits that the practice was expressly forbidden in the Church's Canons of 1604.

It was not sufficient for witches to be condemned as magicians or charmers; they had to be identified as agents and instruments of the Devil. Elizabeth Southerns, or 'Old Demdike' as she was generally known, was the head of a family of witches in Pendle, and was described by Thomas Potts, clerk to the judges at her trial, as: 'a very old woman about the age of fourscore years and had been a Witch for fifty years'. She was also branded as 'a general agent for the Devil in all these parts'. Blamed by her grand-daughter for having made her a witch and accused by her daughter, she was examined by Roger Nowell, a local magistrate, at his home, Read Hall, on 2 April 1612. She confessed what was expected of a witch. On her way home from begging 20 years before, she had met, near a stonepit, in Goldshaw in Pendle: 'a Spirit or Devil in the shape of a boy, the one half of his Coat black, and the other brown, who bade (her)

79

stay, saying to her that if she would give him her soul, she would have anything that she would request'.

The spirit's name was Tibb. Later he appeared to her 'in the likeness of a brown Dog, forcing himself to her knee, to get blood under her left Arm'. Birth marks and other unexplained marks on the body of a suspected witch were always regarded as evidence of intercourse with the Devil. The Devil came in a variety of likenesses — the Pendle witches of 1612 had seen spirits in the form of a man, a dog, a hare and a bear, with a variety of names: Tibb, Fancy, Ball and Dandy. Ann Whittle or 'Chattox', another witch, confessed to have eaten and drunk at a diabolical meal with Demdike and the spirits Tibb and Fancy, but though they ate well 'they were never the fuller nor the better for the same'. Today we tend to explain such stories as creations of the hysterical or deranged mind. Possibly they were fabricated by those who felt that by confessing the existence of pacts with the Devil, they were only living up to what was expected of them and were thus maintaining a certain status, even if it led to death. The confessions were treated seriously enough at the time (especially when supported by the sinister accusations of children), even though some judges were sceptical and, during the course of the seventeenth century, it became harder and harder to find judges who would convict. To maintain that all confessions of consorting with the Devil were fabricated may sound over-sceptical to some, but it must be borne in mind that modern scholars such as Keith Thomas have found no trace of organized Devil-worship in sixteenth- and seventeenth-century England.

That witches were much feared as well as frequently resorted to may be seen by the various anti-witch devices which were intended to protect homes against witches who might harbour some unknown grudge. Special herbs were placed above the threshold, and holed stone amulets were worn as bracelets or necklaces, or placed behind barn or house-doors to protect animals and humans alike. Witch balls like those in the Castle Museum at York were hung in windows to keep out witches and evil spirits. Witch posts, like the one at New House Farm, Rawtenstall, were covered with anti-witch devices and protected doorways. Witch bottles have been discovered at Trawden and elsewhere. These contained the hair or nail-parings mixed with the urine of the victim for whom protection was required, and it was believed that such a device would force the witch to reveal herself, as the effect of the bottle would be to prevent her from passing water. There were undoubtedly many others, but, of all protective devices, probably donkey-stoning of doorsteps — originally to trip up witches — is the one which has survived the longest.

Such devices can be regarded as usual. What was unusual was for local accusations against suspected or known witches to reach the ears of the magistrates and warrant a trial at quarter sessions or assizes. The cause of the trouble seems generally to have been some offence given to the witch by the victim. Refusal of charity was a common grievance, as shown by the case of the Pendle Witches, tried at Lancaster in 1612. The incident which set the whole legal process in motion and sent ten people to the gallows, took place on 18 March 1612 just outside Colne, when John Law, a Halifax pedlar, refused to give pins to Alizon Device, grand-daughter of Old Demdike of Malkin Tower. Alizon was angry with the pedlar, and, almost at once, he had a stroke. Abraham Law, the pedlar's son, took the matter up with the law, and Alizon was charged with witchcraft, which she later admitted. Alizon incriminated members of her own family and that of old Chattox. As each was tried, more stories of retaliatory witchcraft emerged. Demdike, according to Alizon Device, had bewitched to death the child of Richard Baldwin of Weethead because he had not let her on his land. On being chased off she had promised to pray for him and muttered his name 'sundry times'. When Chattox was examined she confessed to having be-witched Anthony Nutter's cow to death, because he had favoured Demdike. The matter might have rested there had not Demdike's family and other local witches met together at Malkin Tower in Pendle on Good Friday. News of the meeting reached Roger Nowell of Read, enquiries were made, and it was concluded that the meeting had been a conspiracy to blow up Lancaster Castle and murder Mr Cowell the gaoler. A total of 19 witches were brought to trial, including some from Samlesbury as well as Pendle. At the trial the evidence of Jennet Device, the nine-year-old grand-daughter of Demdike, was crucial. The ten found guilty of murder were hanged at Golgotha, Lancaster on 20 August 1612.

Witches were usually from the poorer section of the community. One of the condemned Pendle witches, Alice Nutter, described by Potts as a 'rich woman' with 'a great estate and children of good hope', was an exception. She was accused by Elizabeth and James Device of witchcraft and of attending the Malkin Tower meeting, and although she persistently denied her guilt, she was executed

81

along with the rest. We know very little about her circumstances, but it is evident that there was a feud between Chattox and the Nutters, as one of the latter had tried to seduce her daughter. Alice Nutter may have been incriminated in revenge, even though Chattox and her daughter had already bewitched Robert Nutter, the would-be seducer, to death with the aid of 'Fancy'.

Historians seek an explanation for the frequency of clashes between witches and their neighbours in such contemporary changes as the decline of the manorial system, the religious upheavals, the enclosure movement, the increase in population and greater pauperism. In the royal forest of Pendle, where the Crown's control had traditionally been light, rents were stable, although entry fines were increased by James I. A growing population put greater pressure on available land. There were 98 copyholders (or tenants by copy of the manorial roll) in 1527; by 1662 there were 230. It is possible that the enclosure of woodland and waste may have adversely affected the poor and resulted in such tensions as the witch trials reveal, but we cannot be certain. From their frequent accounts of begging expeditions the Malkin Tower witches were obviously poor. A sceptical explanation of their meals with the spirits and the Devil's promises of 'Gold, Silver and Worldly Wealth' must include the possibility that they dreamed of wealth which they had no hope of obtaining.

The Reformation had brought about major changes in the Pendle area. Not only was the church at Newchurch in Pendle built in 1544, bringing the people in closer touch with organized religion than ever before, but from the mid-sixteenth century Puritan influence became strong, through the ministers at Newchurch and the masters at the nearby grammar schools of Clitheroe, Colne, Accrington and Burnley. By the time of the Civil War, the yeomen of Pendle, aggravated by James I's interference with their copyholds and by Charles I's interference with their religion, would be fighting alongside Colonel Richard Shuttleworth of Gawthorpe for the Parliamentary forces.

6 FROM THE CIVIL WAR
TO THE FORTY-FIVE

Lancashire on the eve of the Civil War was a much more prosperous county than a century before. Its tax assessments, compared with other counties, were still low, but most other signs suggest a growing population, a lively commerce and a healthy agriculture. Manchester had grown considerably from migration, and the cloth trade had benefited towns like Bolton and Rochdale. Liverpool had not yet become independent of Chester, but was gaining importance as an alternative point of access to Ireland. Lancaster had enjoyed freedom from Scottish invasion, even if the town had grown little. Preston and Bolton had become centres of trade, as well as of Puritanism. Plague, however, struck in Manchester in 1605 and 1645, and Preston suffered a particularly serious outbreak in 1631, when 1,069 people, about a third of the population, died. This affected the surrounding country area as well, for the commissioners appointed by Charles I to collect money from those who refused royal offers of knighthood, did not enter Amounderness or Lonsdale as they were 'so dangerously infected with the plague'.

Arbitrary taxation of this kind caused much discontent in Lancashire against Charles and his father. Large sums had to be paid by crown tenants who had encroached on the royal forests, and the gentry paid in the form of forced loans and distraint of knighthood. Both merchants and landowners suffered from the imposition of shipmoney — a levy towards upkeep of the navy — between 1636 and 1639, and the whole community was affected when the county had to provide 750 men for service against the Scots in 1638. Puritans became increasingly opposed to the government because of its suspected Roman Catholic leanings, its support of Sunday sports, and its use of the courts of Star Chamber and High Commission, to persecute godly men who did not conform. In the Long Parliament of 1641 which abolished both these courts, there were a number of Lancashire members who voted with Pym and Hampden in opposition to Charles's policies and methods.

When the Civil War broke out, the division between Puritan southeast and Roman Catholic west developed into a political split between the supporters of Parliament and those of the King. Yet civil war cannot occur without a determination to fight, and the early months of the conflict were notable for the efforts of some local leaders to prevent bloodshed. Richard Heyricke, the Puritan Warden of Manchester Collegiate Church, sent a petition with 8,000 signatures to Charles at York, urging him to reach a peaceful settlement with his Parliament. Meanwhile, the recusants, who felt acutely vulnerable to Protestant reprisals after the revolt of the Irish Catholics in 1641, asked the King for permission to defend themselves if attacked.

At Lathom, James Stanley, Lord Strange, shortly to succeed his ageing father as Earl of Derby, was slow to make his position clear. He had attended the King at York in the two Bishops' Wars against the Scots in 1639-40. Parliament seems to have had hopes of his support, for he was named as Lord Lieutenant of Cheshire in a parliamentary list of February 1642. He excused himself from this appointment, however, and accepted the King's commission instead. In spite of his dislike of the royal court and his reluctance to commit himself to either side, Strange once more joined Charles at York and, on his return to Lancashire, held a large royalist demonstration on Fulwood Moor outside Preston. The gathering was attended by about 5,000 people, not all of whom were sympathetic to the King, and who, according to the admittedly hostile account of Alexander Rigby, the local parliamentarian leader, were slow to be convinced.

Hostilities broke out first in Manchester. Lord Strange, who had set up various stores of ammunition at Preston, Warrington, Manchester and Liverpool, during the Scottish campaign, found that the Mancunians would not surrender control of their magazine. An attempt to reach a compromise by holding the magazine jointly in the college buildings next to the church failed. The Manchester apprentices paraded defiantly in the streets. When Lord Strange was invited to a banquet by some of his Manchester friends, he was obliged to abandon the meal and retire to Ordsall Hall, just outside

Salford, followed by a threatening band of the local militia and amid shots from nearby houses. In the commotion, a royalist linen weaver, Richard Perceval, was killed.

Strange determined to return to Manchester in force, but his plans were slow to mature, and by the time he had sent his summons to surrender on 26 September, the defences of Salford bridge and Deansgate were well in hand and the royalist attacks were repulsed. Proposals for a truce were rejected, and on 1 October, Strange, now Earl of Derby, raised the siege.

The failure of the siege and the prospect of a protracted struggle led men on both sides to seek a local peace. Roger Nowell of Read (grandson of the witch-investigator), a royalist captain, but a relative of the parliamentarian Colonel Shuttleworth, and probably encouraged by the earl himself, acted as an intermediary in arranging a meeting between both sides at Blackburn on 13 October 1642. Meanwhile two Cheshire peers hoped to reduce local tension by getting Manchester to disarm its apprentices and take down its fortifications. The threat of popery and the emergency caused by the continuing chaos in Ireland probably helped to harden attitudes, and Mancunians, having won one victory, were not going to give in to the Earl of Derby now. The Blackburn talks collapsed after Parliament issued its veto, and Derby, having failed to take Manchester for the King, went south to meet him at Shrewsbury. He left 'the trayned and freehold bands which were under his commande . . . to be billetted at Warrington and Wigan, and one troope of horse sent to Lathom to defend that house', according to information sent by Ralph Assheton to his friend, Alexander Rigby. It was expected that Derby would soon return to the attack on Manchester, and there were even rumours that the men of Amounderness intended to mutiny and shoot the Earl outside the walls of Manchester in order to end the war in Lancashire.

In fact, the main contribution of Lancashire to the King's cause in 1642 was at the battle of Edgehill. One regiment was led by Sir Thomas Tyldesley of Myerscough, another by Lord Molyneux and Roger Nowell. In Lancashire itself the royalists established themselves in a chain of garrisons around Manchester, in preparation for a spring offensive. Three hundred troops, including two Welsh companies, were stationed at Warrington; another 300 foot, 100 dragoons and a troop of horse at Wigan; 200 men were at Preston, while at Brindle, there was a company under the command of Sir

Gilbert Hoghton, and an outpost at Leigh was manned by 20 men. There was an acute shortage of arms, which meant that other men who might have been mobilized by the gentry remained in reserve. Provisioning of these garrisons was also a problem. Derby tried to prevent profiteering by fixing prices and ordered:

> That Henry Ogle Esquire be Quarter maister generall for bringinge provision to the Army, at reasonable rates, vizt. 3d a pound for butter, 2d ½ pound for cheese, and breade at 16 pound for 12d, hay at 2d a stone to be brought into the severall Garrisons by adiacente townes, and Oates according to the rates of the markett.

Looting was prohibited, and any plunder was to be confiscated and 'disposed for the publicke good'. Meanwhile the enemy, in Manchester, was kept well supplied from north-east Cheshire.

In spite of royalist schemes the forces of Parliament struck first in the New Year of 1643. Receiving news of the weakness of the Preston garrison, Colonel Shuttleworth planned a triple attack from Manchester, Bolton and Blackburn. The 'Manchester men' marched out at night on 12 February, and, according to one parliamentarian author, John Vicars, 'the Lord gave them a fair night to travell in'. They found the town fortified with a double line of brick walls. At first the Preston royalists, armed with pikes, defended the inner works successfully, but the Mancunians under Sir John Seaton forced an entry at the end of Church Street. In the fierce fighting that followed, the Mayor of Preston, Adam Mort, and his son were both killed, along with a Roman Catholic physician called Westby. After two hours the town surrendered. A number of prominent royalists were taken prisoner, but Towneley of Towneley and Sir Gilbert Hoghton managed to escape to Wigan.

The year continued as badly as it had begun for the King's supporters in Lancashire. Although the Earl of Derby soon retook Preston, he failed to take Lancaster Castle and set fire to the town in revenge. The little houses with their thatched roofs were soon ablaze, and it was years before Lancaster fully recovered. In April, Derby was defeated by Assheton at Whalley and was obliged to surrender Wigan and Warrington. Trouble on his island of Man forced him to abandon the summer campaign on the mainland, and while he was away on Man, the parliamentary forces captured Liverpool, retook Preston and won control of the Lune Valley by taking Hornby and Thurland Castles. By the end of 1643 only Lathom House and Greenhalgh Castle remained in royalist hands.

Parliamentarian successes in the north-west were temporarily jeopardized by Newcastle's victory over their West Riding allies at Adwalton Moor in June 1643, but the contingent of Manchester men who had gone to help managed to retire from the battle intact and successfully fortified Rochdale and Blackstone Edge against any royalist attack from the east. The local parliamentarian successes were rounded off by the defeat of the first detachments of the King's troops from Ireland at Nantwich in January 1644. This victory by the Manchester men under Sir Thomas Fairfax ended Charles's last hope of breaking the military deadlock in the approaches to London.

A flying campaign by Prince Rupert in the early summer of 1644 temporarily improved the King's fortunes in the north-west. Rupert, accompanied by Derby, who had wintered with the King at Oxford, stormed through Cheshire with 8,000 men and 50 pieces of ordnance. Stockport fell, and Manchester seemed threatened, but Sir John Meldrum who commanded its defence had 5,000 foot soldiers at his disposal, and Rupert was more concerned to make a brilliant display and ensure that Liverpool was safe for royal transports, than to get bogged down in the siege of Manchester. Skirting that town, the prince fell upon Bolton. The town was defended by Colonel Rigby and the force which had lately been undertaking the siege of Lathom. They were no match for the prince's army. The sack of Bolton on 27 May 1644 was one of the grimmest incidents of the whole war and provides ample illustration of the ruthless streak in Rupert's generalship. The exact numbers of killed and wounded are not known and may have been exaggerated, but Bolton had still not recovered when, nine years later, it presented a 'humble petition (for relief) of the poore widdowes, Maymed Souldiers and Fatherles Childeren, whose husbands or parents were slayne att the surprizall of Boulton by Prince Rupert'.

From Bolton, Rupert marched to Wigan and on to Liverpool, his primary objective. There the parliamentarian garrison under Colonel John Moore took to sea after four days' intensive cannonade. At Lathom, Rupert and his force were entertained for a week by the Earl and Countess of Derby, before setting off once more up the Ribble Valley to Yorkshire where he intended to raise the siege of

York. While he had met no real resistance in Lancashire, York was another matter, and he was there out-generalled by Fairfax and Cromwell at the battle of Marston Moor.

Rupert's gains in Lancashire did not last long. The parliamentarians quickly recovered the lost ground and once more returned to the siege of Lathom House. After Marston Moor the Earl and Countess took refuge on the Isle of Man, but their household continued to hold out. Royalist weakness for the first time took the pressure off Manchester, and Assheton led his regiment of foot in the ranks of Cromwell's New Model Army which finally shattered the King's cause at the battle of Naseby in June 1645. Lathom surrendered on 3 December 1645, after receiving the King's instructions for the surrender of isolated garrisons. Sir Thomas Tyldesley, Governor of Lichfield, also surrendered on royal orders, but not until July 1646, two months after Charles himself had surrendered to the Scots army at Newark.

The end of the Civil War could only be greeted with relief in Lancashire. Certain areas had suffered badly. Lancaster had been destroyed by fire; Bolton had been sacked; 360 had been killed in Prince Rupert's attack on Liverpool, including 'one poor blind man', in spite of promises of free quarter. Preston had changed hands three times; so too had Wigan and the town was to be the scene of more fighting in 1648 and 1651. When Colonel Rosworm took the town for Parliament in March 1643, his soldiers ransacked it, dragging great heaps of cloth out into the streets, and seizing 'treasure' to the value of £20,000, which local farmers and gentry had entrusted to the garrison for safe-keeping. The church was looted, and the town records were thrown into the street. Wigan was again plundered in 1648, this time by Scottish soldiers. Not surprisingly, the mayor and aldermen were petitioning the City of London in 1649 for relief from the 'three-corded scourge of sword, pestilence and famine'.

The 'pestilence', or plague, was a recurring menace which now seemed the last straw. Several towns were affected by outbreaks. At Liverpool Rupert had observed the great number of rats leaving the ships at low water and running 'in troops into the town for provisions, and so back again towards flood'. Plague hit Manchester badly at the end of the war. Between June and October 1645, 995 burials were recorded in the register of the Collegiate Church.

The effect of the war on an 'ordinary' Lancastrian may be seen from the life of Adam Martindale. Aged 19 when the war broke out,

Martindale saw its effect on his father's building business:

> The great trade that my father and two of my brethren had long driven was quite dead; for who would build or repair an house when he could not sleep a night in it with quiet and safety?

The Martindale family was Puritan and lived in the 'no man's land' between Manchester and Lathom. Adam's mind was made up for him by the activities of the royalist recruiting-sergeants in the Prescot area. He was appalled by the way old country people, armed only with pitchforks, were obliged to join the Earl of Derby's attack on Bolton, strengthened at the rear by: 'troopers that had commission to shoot such as lagged behind'. This was enough to send his brother Henry off to Bolton after them, but to join the defence not the attack. Adam, too, was reluctant to join the royalists, partly on account of his Puritan upbringing. He wrote: 'I could not clear myself from it by swearing and debauchery, but would (rather) have been quiet and meddled on no side'. He too joined the round-heads, as a clerk to Colonel Moore, the commander of the Liverpool garrison. At Liverpool, Adam soon found that parliamentarian language and behaviour was no better than royalist. His resolution was strengthened by news that his father's house had been plundered and their cattle driven off by Prince Rupert's soldiers. The remnant of the family assets disappeared when his father lent a large sum of money to a Roman Catholic whose possessions had all been seques-tered by Parliament. Later Adam found a comfortable living as schoolmaster and minister; not everyone in the battle areas of south Lancashire was so fortunate.

The surrender of Lathom in 1645 was not the end of fighting in Lancashire. In 1648 the second Civil War broke out. A Scottish army of 24,000 men under the Duke of Hamilton invaded the north-west of England on behalf of Charles I, on the understanding that he would introduce the Presbyterian form of church government south of the border. These negotiations did not affect loyalties in Lancashire, and Ralph Assheton mustered a force to resist the Scots, while Sir Thomas Tyldesley and other royalists prepared to support them. The invasion of the north-west took the English Parliament by surprise. The vanguard of the large Scottish army had reached Preston before Cromwell was in a position to intercept it. With a much smaller but better co-ordinated force, he raced over the Pennines by way of Skipton, reaching Clitheroe on 16 August. The next day he struck Hamilton's left flank, composed of English royalists under Sir Marmaduke Langdale, outside Preston, on Fulwood and Ribbleton Moors. After a 'very sharp dispute, continuing three or four hours' — as Cromwell wrote afterwards — Langdale's troops were defeated and large supplies of arms taken. That evening the roundheads pursued the Scots up to the Ribble at Walton bridge.

During the next two days, a running battle was fought between Cromwell, supported by Assheton, and the Scots as they straggled along between Preston and Warrington. The skirmishes, notably on Standish Moor, resulted in a Scottish rout, and several thousand surrendered at Warrington Bridge. Small groups of Scots scattered through the countryside, only to find that 'the Country people rise and knock them in the head' — according to one report. Besides arms and ammunition, Cromwell captured important correspondence between Hamilton and Prince Charles, as well as '500 cattle retaken that they had plundered from the Country'. No wonder that 'the poor country people' were 'overjoyed at this great deliverance', if it meant the return of their cattle. Hamilton was taken prisoner in Shropshire and executed in 1649, only two months after his King.

Three years after the battle of Preston, a second Scottish army invaded Lancashire, this time in the name of the dead King's son and heir, Charles, Prince of Wales. The Earl of Derby abandoned his six-year exile at Castle Rushen on the Isle of Man and landed in the Wyre estuary on 15 August 1651, to raise Lancashire for the new King. With him was that veteran royalist soldier, Sir Thomas Tyldesley. Recruitment in the Fylde and at Lathom raised Derby's force from 300 to 1,500, but he had no success in his attempt to win support at Warrington or Preston. On his return from Preston to Warrington, his force was destroyed in Wigan Lane by a regiment under General John Lambert, the parliamentarian commander in the north. Sir Thomas Tyldesley was killed, but Derby himself, although wounded, managed to get away. Charles and the Scots were defeated in their turn at the battle of Worcester, eight days later on 2 September.

Once more Lancashire churches were used as temporary military prisons. At Walton the forms and windows were smashed, and at Manchester Henry Newcome recorded that 'the poor imprisoned Scots' left much 'nastiness'. Soon after the disaster at Worcester Derby was captured near Nantwich. He was court-martialled at Chester, found guilty of high treason, and condemned to die at Bolton. He attempted to escape from Chester Castle, was caught and later taken to Bolton for execution. On the scaffold he declared his innocence:

> . . . it was said that I was a man accustomed to be a man of Blood, But it doth not lie upon my Conscience for I was wrongfully belied. I thank God I did 'desire peace. I was born in honour, I lived in honour, and I hope I shall die with honour . . .

His death signified the end of the quasi-feudal power exerted by his predecessors although his failure to win Lancashire for the King had shown that this stranglehold had already been broken. His widow, Charlotte, surrendered the Isle of Man a month after her husband's execution and she remained there as a prisoner. Their son, Charles, took part in Sir George Booth's abortive rising at Warrington in 1658. At the Restoration in 1660, his mother was released and he got back his father's estates as the eighth earl. His dead father acquired the title of 'the martyr earl'.

Oliver Cromwell died in 1658, and Charles II was enthroned unconditionally in 1660. In Lancashire the Restoration was greeted with relief. It marked the end of the search for alternative sources of authority in church and state. It also meant the end of the power of the army and its interference in local affairs, particularly in the question of morals and traditional pastimes. Charles's coronation was celebrated by a big service of thanksgiving at Manchester Collegiate Church, presided over by that elderly Puritan, Richard Heyricke. His enthusiasm and that of many other Presbyterian supporters of monarchy quickly turned to disappointment. The Clarendon Code not only restored the bishops, church courts and the Book of Common Prayer, but also included the Five Mile and Conventicle Acts, designed to curb the preaching and teaching of those ministers who had preferred to resign their livings rather than abandon their ideals of church government.

One Lancashire Presbyterian who felt unable to conform to the Restoration Church was Henry Newcome, the popular minister who had assisted Heyricke at Manchester between 1657 and 1662. When the college of clergy was reconstituted, Heyricke was reappointed Warden, but the new fellows were hostile to Newcome. The latter wrote in his diary: 'The fellows oft in this time expressed their disgust to me behind my back, and professedly said I should not preach unless I would conform.' Newcome was not made a fellow, but hoped to be able to continue merely preaching 'to win souls to God'. This he did throughout 1661, in spite of a recurrence of fits for which he had to be bled. He preached, for example, to the 'townsmen at their fair', on the subject of drinking toasts. The practice of drinking people's health had died during the Commonwealth but revived with the Restoration. Newcome's sermon certainly had its effect, for no-one dared give a toast at that townsmen's dinner. From 1662, however, he had to give up public preaching, and in 1664, his private services were threatened by the Conventicle Act. Even though few Manchester people would have betrayed him, the Bishop of Chester was well aware that Newcome was likely to hold such meetings. In 1664, for the first time, he was not invited to preach at the Manchester town dinner, although, suppressing his 'envy and anger', he went as Sir Edward Mosley's guest. Such a friendship, and, even more, that of Lord Delamere and the Hoghtons, was to be one of Newcome's chief assets at a time when the leadership of the Lancashire Presbyterians was being weakened by death and changed circumstances.

In spite of his Puritan background, Newcome reacted favourably to the more liberal attitude to sports which characterized the Restoration. He had been nutting on the Sabbath as a boy, and continued to play bandy-ball (a type of tennis) with his family on Sundays. He was also fond of a game of shuffleboard (or shovelboard), but disliked the heavy drinking which so often went with it. He does not even seem to have objected, in principle, to the revival of the Shrove Tuesday custom, condemned as much by Puritans as by Bishop Oldham, which allowed school-children the day off for sports and cock-fighting. Newcome was more worried by the dangers to children of flying arrows: 'I understood I had cause, for (his son) Daniel's hat on his head was shot through with an arrow'.

The Great Plague hit London in 1665. Manchester was not affected that year, but Newcome 'kept a day in private for poor London', and gave a talk based on Paul's advice to Christians in prison from the epistle to the Hebrews. Those who could avoided London that summer.

Newcome's wife had a 'distemper' so, in 1665 and again in the following year, he took her to Scarborough for a cure. They travelled on horseback with two cousins and broke the journey at Leeds:

June 16th 1665 We came to Scarborough about four o'clock. We found mercy and a providence in that we sent the night before,

92

FROM THE CIVIL WAR TO THE FORTY-FIVE

for the doctor otherwise had been gone to York this day, and so we had his company and counsel to set in to the use of the waters.

They rented 'two neat rooms' from a merchant and were pleased to be allowed to eat on their own for only 8d (3½p) a meal. Of the other members of the party, one suffered from 'emerods', another from 'sad epileptic fits'. When they got back to Manchester they found 'the smallpox prevailing greatly in the town, and very mortal'. Two of their neighbours had lost children in the epidemic.

The Five Mile Act obliged Newcome to leave Manchester, and he and his wife took up lodgings with a friend who lived outside the town. At Dunham, the home of Lord Delamere, Newcome met a former Warrington minister who had been similarly exiled. The Act did not prevent Newcome visiting his friends and family and praying with them, albeit illegally. The arrival of the 'chimney lookers' to assess homes for the hearth tax gave him a shock, but he was not discovered. He took his troubles with a good grace. He was undoubtedly less worried by statutory restrictions on dissenting ministers like himself than by the threat of a Roman Catholic uprising or St Bartholomew's massacre in England.

Henry Newcome also had more practical problems to face. He was short of money and had several sons to launch into the world. In 1668 he set about finding an apprenticeship for his son, Daniel. At first he arranged with a London glover, the brother of a Cambridge friend. But the glover was not 'careful for religion', and Newcome quickly realized that he would not have the capital to set his son up in business as a glover after the seven years were complete. Instead, Dan was apprenticed to a ribbon factor at Blackwall Hall. To the Puritan mind, a career in ribbons was not ideal, but Newcome's conscience was salved by the factor's insistence on 'catechising and sabbath keeping and constant business' in the training of his young apprentice. Indeed he seems to have been a little too rigorous. He would not let Dan have an extra gown in winter, and Dan had in fact been advised by another boy in the same house not to agree to be bound as apprentice. The adults, however, prevailed, and Newcome wrote in his diary: 'December 18th, we sealed the bonds and covenants, and all things were smooth and well; and, December 16th, (Saturday) we were all invited to his master's house to dinner, and exceeding much made of'.

The apprenticeship did not go the full term, for, two years later,

Dan ran away. He was found and brought back to his master. Newcome went to London by coach to see them. It was concluded that 'vile knaves' had 'made a prey' of the lad, but his apprenticeship was not renewed. When Newcome had settled with the factor he decided that the only alternative was for Dan to try his luck in the colonies. So he was put on board a ship belonging to a merchant friend, bound for Jamaica by way of Tangier. Dan got cold feet on the voyage and wrote home to say he feared he was likely to be sold as an indentured servant. Such fears proved to be unfounded, but, on arrival in Jamaica, Dan contracted yellow fever and returned to England.

Henry Newcome's hopes soared when Charles II announced his Declaration of Indulgence in 1672 by which Roman Catholics and Protestant dissenters were granted full freedom of worship and assembly. He at once began to preach publicly in his house and in a local barn. The Declaration, however, was unpopular, and Newcome was summoned before the magistrates for his activities. He showed them his licence to preach, under the Indulgence, and so nothing more was said. After ten months' freedom, the King revoked the Declaration at the insistence of the House of Commons. Newcome and his fellow dissenters were bitterly disappointed, but the news of the cancellation was regarded as a triumph in Manchester. Newcome wrote: 'It was entertained with great joy in the town, with bells and bonfires, under the notion of the King and parliament being agreed . . . (there is) much joy and scorn over us.' Financial difficulties once more became acute, especially as two of his sons were of university age. Fortunately, his brothers were comfortably off, and, with their help, his sons' education was not curtailed.

Political troubles intensified in the 1680s. In 1683 and 1685 all dissenters came under suspicion for complicity in the Rye House Plot against Charles II and the Monmouth Rebellion against his Roman Catholic brother and successor James II. Newcome's house was searched on both occasions, but nothing incriminating was found. Lord Delamere was put on trial for treason in 1686, but acquitted. The following year, James II's Declaration of Indulgence gave Newcome a new opportunity for preaching in public.

The revolution of 1688 and the accession of William and Mary to the English throne took everyone by surprise, except those members of the aristocracy who had planned it. In Manchester Newcome and his friends were amazed by James II's sudden departure, and took great interest in the war in Ireland where at first James's supporters had the upper hand. So much was the Irish campaign on Newcome's mind that one night he cried out in his sleep for the Protestants besieged in Londonderry: 'It is, I hope, no presage of any danger they are in more than ordinary'. The defeat of James II in Ireland was a relief to Newcome and many other Lancashire Protestants. The Toleration Act of 1689, following the Bill of Rights, at last gave dissenters the statutory right to hold public services. And in 1693 Newcome's congregation built him a handsome meeting-house in Cross Street. He could not enjoy it for long, for he died on 17 September 1695.

A man whose religious views and daily concerns were very different from those of Henry Newcome was Nicholas Blundell of Little Crosby. Born in 1669, a generation after Newcome, he, like most of his neighbours, was anxious to forget the struggles of the past. Blundell came from an old Roman Catholic family which had held the manor of Little Crosby, near Liverpool, since 1362. There were many other Roman Catholic gentry in south-west Lancashire and between them they maintained the 'old faith' in the area. Blundell himself had a brother who was a priest and five of his six sisters were nuns. Jesuits and missionaries were constantly at Little Crosby Hall; his tenants were mainly Roman Catholics and Mass, although illegal, was often celebrated in one of his barns.

Nicholas Blundell, like the other Roman Catholic gentry, was on very good terms with his Protestant neighbours. He dined occasionally with the Earl of Derby at Lathom and frequently with the local Protestant clergy, particularly the Master of Crosby Grammar School. Anglicans and Roman Catholics, squires and tenants, formed a bowling club. Bowls were followed by talking, drinking and cards late into the night. Yet there were still some echoes of the hostility at national level. Jacobite plots put good relations at risk, and one or two Protestant clergy kept their ears to the ground for information against Roman Catholics.

Nicholas Blundell spent most of his time running his family estate. He was very keen on the best methods of cultivation both traditional and modern. Marling had been used for improving Lancashire's sandy soils since at least the twelfth century, and Blundell ensured that his tenants marled and manured the fields. He discussed the 'Beyond-sea' (or Dutch) manner of feeding livestock with his chaplain and introduced clover as well as various types of corn seed.

He docked the tails of his sheep, because ' 'tis said they feed the better for it'. When visitors came to Little Crosby he showed them his cattle and pigs with great pride. Blundell took an interest in the new science of surveying and set about making his own map of Little Crosby. He enjoyed experimenting as much in the brewhouse and kitchen as in the fields. He brewed Brunswick beer or 'Mumm', and in June 1705, 'tryed an experimenting with eleven Miss (mice) in a Hot Pot'! In the following year he was making improvements to the Hall by adding a parlour with the latest sash-windows and laying out a lawn with flowerbeds and fruit trees. The surplus fruit was sold to hucksters from Liverpool.

Legal business took him to Liverpool, Lancaster and Preston. At Liverpool he bought clothes and furniture, pills and medicines. Some special items were sent from Chester, such as glass for the windows of his coach. He bought a periwig of horsehair from 'a woman that came past my gates'. On other occasions a tailor came out from Liverpool 'to mend my Wives Stayes' and a tinker came to the door and mended three frying pans.

Nicholas Blundell was a benevolent landlord, as well as a strict one. He and his wife visited their tenants and humbler neighbours in their homes and cottages — often with a charitable motive: 'My wife rode behind me to the North End to Condole Ailes Tickle for the Death of her Son John . . . ' At times he gave money, sometimes he just lent a helping hand: 'I gave Margarit Riding 18d. I found Richard Harrisons Bullock in the Ditch and helped to pull him out'. He lent his horses to servants and tenants alike, if their need was sufficiently great, and he lent his greyhounds to his gardener for coursing. At traditional festivals he kept open house for his neighbours at Little Crosby. There was often dancing to fiddles, and plenty of home-brewed ale was provided. On 29 February 1706 he recorded: 'Some good Wives came to turn Pankakes. Wm. Thelwall & Pat. Gelibrond (a priest) drunk in the Gallery . . . ' (F. Tyrer, *The Great Diurnall of Nicholas Blundell*)

Nicholas Blundell enjoyed a great variety of sports; coursing hares was a particular favourite, but he liked skating, shooting and horse-racing too. He attended horse-races at Great Crosby, on Liverpool Sands and occasionally at Ormskirk. In February 1704 'I went to Ormskirk Cocking, it being the second days fighting for a Plate. Mr Blundell of Ince won it.' The Disbursement Book tells us that he lost 8s 0d (40p) in this fight but took his losses well, for four days later: 'I went to congratulate Cozen Blundell for winning a Plate at the Cocking at Ormskirk'.

Even his courtship was businesslike and methodical. Nicholas Blundell was almost 33 when he succeeded to the family estate in 1702. He was not yet married, but by the following spring he was taking steps to remedy this. On 28 February 1703 he went over to Scarisbrick to discuss with his cousin Robert 'my going to Hathrop', in Oxfordshire, the home of his future bride, Frances, daughter of Marmaduke, third Lord Langdale of Holme. His cousin must have encouraged him, for a few days after his visit to Scarisbrick he was writing to Frances's grandmother, Lady Webb. The letter was given to Walter Thelwall, Blundell's most trusted servant, who set off for Heythrop on 4 March and was back with a reply eight days later. Blundell immediately wrote to Lord Langdale to arrange the dowry and to Lord Molyneux for his approval, and on 6 April he heard from Lady Webb that he might wait on 'Mrs' Frances Langdale as soon as he pleased. In preparation for the journey he ordered a black coat from his Liverpool tailor and armed himself in case of attack. A week later he set out for Heythrop. After travelling steadily for five days and four nights he arrived safely at his destination.

The courtship was brief and to the point. On his second day at Heythrop he had talks with both Lord Langdale and Lady Webb and made his 'first address to Mrs Frances Langdale'. Nothing of note passed on the third day, but events soon began to move swiftly:

> 21 April Lady Webb discoursed me in the Garden I discoursed Mrs Langdale in the Kitchen Garden . . . 22 April Mrs Morgan dined at Heythrop. Mr Morgan and I discoursed of Cattle & Sheep &c: Lady Dowager Webb Read the Heads of Agreement of Marriage to be between Mrs Frances Langdale & me N: Bl: in Presence of Lord Langdale & Sr John Webb.

A lawyer was summoned to draw up the Heads of Articles of Marriage and these were signed on 25 April. On 28 April Blundell, who had recorded no further conversation with his future wife in his diary, presented her with an engagement ring — described in his accounts as a 'Fals Diamond Ring 14s 0d'. On 3 May Blundell went to London to see the sights and attend the theatre, and later he made a second trip to buy a wedding ring (£1 5s 0d) and a wedding suit, and to transact other business. On 17 June he records baldly in his diary:

'I was married to Lord Langdales Daughter by Mr Slaughter a Clergyman'. A week later he sent home for his 'chariot' and on 2 July he brought his new wife home to Crosby.

The whole transaction had been accomplished in a little under three months. Blundell had got what he wanted, namely a Roman Catholic bride of noble birth with a dowry of £2,000. The marriage appears to have been not unsuccessful. The couple had two daughters and, although his strong-willed wife could get across friends, relatives and servants, there is no hint of unhappiness between them. Such a marriage, founded on convenience but built into a happy relationship over the years, must have been typical of many in the eighteenth century.

The war of 1689-94, between William III and James II, produced only minor ripples in Lancashire, in spite of the fact that it had the largest Roman Catholic population of any English county. In 1671 there were 5,496 convicted recusants in Lancashire, and many were still grouped in enclaves around such manor houses as Little Crosby, scattered throughout the western and northern districts of the county. James II's abrupt departure in 1688 and the failure of his campaigns in Scotland and Ireland did not inspire confidence in Lancashire's Roman Catholics. Some sympathy for James undoubtedly existed, but no evidence of active support was found when eight of their leading gentlemen, including Lord Molyneux and Nicholas Blundell's father, were tried for treason on charges brought by an informer named John Lunt. The 'Lancashire Plot' of 1694 turned out to be Lunt's own invention.

The death of Queen Anne in 1714 and Bolingbroke's last-minute decision to support the long-rejected claim of James II's son, the Old Pretender, sparked off a major Jacobite revolt in Scotland and the north of England. At George I's proclamation there was a riot in Manchester led by a Jacobite called Tom Syddall, and although the Lancashire boroughs sent loyal addresses to the new King, some of the county's Roman Catholic gentry were in touch with Jacobites in Northumberland. In October 1715 a force was raised in that county under Thomas Forster, one of the Members of Parliament and it set out to raise recruits in the borders. Joined by Clan Chattan under Brigadier McIntosh at Kelso, Forster turned south to try his luck in Lancashire where one of his lieutenants, Lord Widdrington, had many relatives.

Resistance to the Jacobites was nominal in Cumberland and

Westmorland, and on 7 November James III was proclaimed King in the Market Square, Lancaster, after the abandonment of a half-hearted attempt to impede the Jacobites' progress by dismantling the bridge over the Lune. At Lancaster, Forster and McIntosh were joined by a number of north Lancashire gentry including John Dalton of Thurnham Hall and Albert Hodgson of Leighton Hall. Sir Henry Hoghton of Hoghton Tower, the commander of the Hanoverian forces in north Lancashire, feared damage to property by the Jacobites and recommended the locals to defend their livelihoods if threatened, but no damage was reported and no resistance offered. Even Christopher Hopkins, the Lancaster stationer, who was caught counting the numbers of rebel troops, was treated lightly.

At Preston, which the Jacobites reached on 9 and 10 November, there was something of a party atmosphere. The town was crowded not only with the Scottish and Northumbrian troops, but also with local Roman Catholic gentlemen like Richard Towneley of Towneley (Lord Widdrington's brother-in-law), Edward Tyldesley of Myerscough, and Sir Francis Anderton of Anderton, who had arrived to entertain and support their friends and relatives. The reunions did not last long, as almost immediately General Wills was reported to be approaching from Wigan and General Carpenter from Barnard Castle. The Jacobites had no scheme by which to defeat the advancing Hanoverian forces. Instead they erected four defence-barriers at the ends of Church Street, Lancaster Road, Friargate and Fishergate, and waited to be attacked. General Wills opened his attack first on the Church Street, and then on the Friargate barriers in the afternoon of Saturday, 12 November. The next morning General Carpenter arrived from Clitheroe, and, after an offer of safe conduct, and much argument between Englishmen and Highlanders, Forster at last surrendered at 7 pm on 13 November. On the same day the Jacobites under the Earl of Mar suffered defeat at the battle of Sheriffmuir. At Preston the Jacobite officers were imprisoned in the inns, while the rank and file — mainly Highlanders — were herded into the parish church after laying down their arms in the market place.

Many of the ordinary Jacobites were imprisoned or transported. Forty-three of their leaders, including Tom Syddall, were executed, mainly at Preston, but also at Garstang, Lancaster, Liverpool, Wigan and Manchester. Four were executed at Tyburn. Some of the gentry were acquitted, including Richard Towneley; Sir Francis Anderton forfeited his lands, and Richard Sherburne and George Clifton were outlawed. John Dalton was imprisoned and fined.

As a result of the Fifteen, all Roman Catholics of importance were suspected of disloyalty. Nicholas Blundell of Little Crosby, being related to Lord Widdrington through his wife's brother, stayed at home as much as possible in the first two weeks of November. On the Sunday of Forster's surrender at Preston his house was twice searched for arms by foot-soldiers from Liverpool. None were found, but the Blundells took no chances. Nicholas's wife hid the 'mass things' in the attic, and on 24 November she and her husband went off on an extended visit to London, Douai and Rome which kept them away from Crosby until the autumn of 1717. By that time the feeling against Roman Catholics had died down and Blundell was able to resume his friendly relations with local Protestants.

After the experience of the Fifteen, Lancashire Jacobites were naturally more reluctant to take part in the rebellion led by the Young Pretender against George II in 1745. The Highland Jacobites followed the same route into Lancashire as their predecessors and found the same absenteeism and apathy among the Protestant authorities as had the Jacobite forces in the Fifteen. Jacobite recruitment, however, was not nearly so successful. Francis Towneley was the only important recruit to join the Young Pretender at Preston on 27 November and this time there was little response in Manchester. Once again Lancashire had failed to come up to Jacobite expectations. Charles moved on to Derby, but was back in Manchester in full retreat, by 9 December. The advance guard arrived at Lancaster on 13 December, and the Duke of Perth freed the Jacobite stragglers who had been rounded up and imprisoned in Lancaster Castle. On the following day the main army arrived, and while the soldiers were fitted out with new clothes by local tailors and shoemakers, the officers attended an organ recital in the parish church. The Jacobites left the town on 15 December with General Oglethorpe and his dragoons hard on their heels.

The aftermath of the Forty-Five was less serious for Lancashire Roman Catholic gentry than that of the Fifteen. Only the Towneleys really suffered. Sir John Towneley followed the Young Pretender to France, while his younger brother Francis, who had been left to hold Carlisle against the advance of the Duke of Cumberland, was executed in London, in spite of his plea of holding a French commission. Many ordinary Jacobite soldiers were imprisoned in

100

Lancaster Castle where 80 died of typhus. In Liverpool a Protestant mob took revenge on local Roman Catholics by destroying their chapel.

In both the Fifteen and the Forty-Five it is difficult not to be struck by the unity and homogeneity of Lancashire society in spite of religious division. The main attitude of Roman Catholics and Protestants alike to the Jacobite rebellion was one of apathy and avoidance. Sir Henry Hoghton's task of arousing local resistance was about as thankless as Bishop Nicholson's at Carlisle. Coping with the Jacobites was a job for the professional soldier. Individuals were willing to 'have a go', like Dr Henry Bracken of Lancaster in 1745, who rounded up Jacobite stragglers, but most men of property kept well out of the way.

An exceptional group reaction was that of the dissenters. To them a Jacobite victory presented the possibility of an end to toleration under the Act of 1689, and even the wholesale destruction of Protestantism. In immediate terms, the Jacobite mob in Manchester meant the destruction of their homes and meeting-houses. The Reverend James Woods, a minister at Chowbent, determined to take action, and in the Fifteen he led his congregation, armed with agricultural implements, to Walton-le-Dale where, under General Wills's instructions he lined them up on the south bank of the Ribble safely out of harm's way, but near enough to the action to share in the Jacobites' defeat.

In the Forty-Five the dissenters had less opportunity to demonstrate their loyalty to the Hanoverians. Fervent prayers were made for deliverance from 'the Hands of wicked and unreasonable men' and from 'the Nursling from Rome' (a reference to Bonnie Prince Charlie). 'Having never seen the Rebells, or any in a Highland Dress' one dissenting doctor, John Kay of Bury, went to watch the retreat from Manchester to Wigan and then went on to Manchester to 'hear how the Rebells behaved themselves there'. On the following two days it was with great relief that he recorded seeing 'a great many of our Majesty King George's forces pass through Manchester pursuing the Rebells from Scotland'. As for behaviour, the Jacobite troops in Lancashire showed far more self-discipline and consideration for the local population than the Hanoverian troops in Scotland were to show after their victory at Culloden.

7 THE INDUSTRIAL REVOLUTION

Liverpool at the accession of King George III was a thriving seaport, with a population approaching 30,000. By 1801 the town's population was over 75,000, and it was well established as one of the largest ports in the kingdom.

Liverpool's prosperity derived from its trade with Ireland, Africa and the Americas. In the early eighteenth century a growing volume of tobacco and sugar was imported, while the major exports were cloth — both woollen and cotton — salt and coal. Its coastal trade was vitally important for the collection and distribution of goods and the growth of overseas and coastal trades encouraged the improvement of inland communications. The river Weaver, made more navigable in the 1720s, brought salt; the Sankey Canal, completed in 1757, brought coal. Turnpike roads to Prescot and Warrington facilitated the movement of earthenware goods and precision instruments such as watches. The completion of the Grand Trunk (Trent–Mersey) Canal in 1777 brought Wedgwood pottery and Birmingham smallwares; the Bridgewater Canal carried Worsley coal and Manchester cottons. There was little in the way of manufacture in Liverpool itself, although the town was an important centre for many processing trades. In 1784 Dr W. Moss, a local surgeon, pointed out that Liverpool's atmosphere was laden with smoke and 'effluvia' from works where salt, hides, whale-oil, sugar and tobacco were treated. On the other hand he thought that the smoke from the tobacco refineries and the sulphur fumes from the copper works were positively advantageous to the health of the inhabitants.

It was a three-day journey to Liverpool by stagecoach from

London in 1760 and seven days by waggon. The coach put down its passengers, jolted into a state of exhaustion, at one of the principal inns. Samuel Derrick, writing to the Earl of Cork, told him of three good inns in Liverpool where 'for tenpence a man dines elegantly at an ordinary (meal) consisting of ten or a dozen dishes'. Derrick wrote with approval of the mutton, fowl and fish that he had sampled at one. This was appropriate fare for a man wealthy enough to afford the £2 6s 0d (£2.30) for an inside seat in the 'Flying Machine'. By 1796 the *Liverpool Guide* could mention a hotel and four or five inns, as well as a variety of taverns. By that date the Royal Mail coaches were in operation, and the journey between London and Liverpool had been reduced to 27 hours.

The great attraction of Liverpool was its docks. Two wet docks had been built by 1760 and four more had been completed by 1796. These new docks were built for specific purposes. The Salthouse Dock of 1753 was designed principally for the Cheshire salt trade, while the Duke's Dock, completed in 1773, served the coal traffic from the Bridgewater mines at Worsley. Three new docks, opened in 1771, 1788 and 1796, were built to cater for the expanding West Indies and American trades in sugar and cotton. Between 1811 and 1825 the dock acreage almost doubled, and even that total of 51 acres was to be quadrupled by 1860. The Old Dock, which reached into the heart of the town, had been converted from the 'pool' by the engineer, Thomas Steers, between 1709 and 1715. It was dominated by the Custom House, the headquarters of the town's trade, which stood at its east end. A variety of vessels might have been seen in the dock in the 1760s, the smaller ones engaged in the coastal and Irish trades, the larger ships — perhaps two or three hundred tons — in overseas trade with Virginia or the West Indies. Here, too, a packet boat might be boarded for Ireland, just as John Wesley did with his chaise in 1773. His boat ran aground in the Mersey, and he had to re-embark the next day. The year before, Thomas Earle founded the first overseas packet line, between Liverpool and Leghorn in Italy.

Daniel Defoe had commented that Liverpool was unrivalled in the provinces for 'the fineness of the streets and the beauty of the buildings'. A visitor in 1760 would have admired the houses in Paradise and Hanover Streets which belonged to the 'Africa merchants' as the men who financed the slave trade were known. In the 1760s housing began to stretch south-eastwards towards Wolstenholme

Square and along Duke Street. Part of an old ropery had been converted into Ladies Walk. In 1768 Richard Kent, a wealthy merchant, gave a grand entertainment to celebrate the completion of his new mansion at the corner of Duke and Kent streets. By 1796 Rodney Street had been laid out on the higher ground which Dr Moss had described as the healthiest part of the town. It was there in 1809 that the wife of the slave-owning planter and merchant, John Gladstone, gave birth to the future Liberal Prime Minister, William Ewart Gladstone.

Liverpool was rapidly developing as an important social centre for people with money in the mid-eighteenth century. The theatre built in 1759 in Drury Lane was where Prescot-born John Philip Kemble first trod the boards with his sister Sarah (later Mrs Siddons). Samuel Derrick, the Master of Ceremonies at Bath, impressed by the Assembly Room in the Town Hall (completed 1754), described it as 'grand, spacious and finely illuminated'. Meetings were held fortnightly, in season, for dancing and card-playing, at which a lady styled 'the queen' presided and where, as Derrick drily observed, 'some women' were 'elegantly accomplished and perfectly well dressed'.

Derrick found the merchants who discussed business at the exchange or in one of the coffee houses friendly, hospitable, and even adequately genteel. For his part, he liked the abundance of rum to be found in Liverpool. Liverpool merchants, unlike the inhabitants of Bath, were men of business. Much of their spare cash went into the financing of docks and canals, although they also earned a reputation for philanthropy in the endowment of the Bluecoat School and the Infirmary, not to mention the large number of new churches. John Gladstone alone built three churches between 1815 and 1840.

The whole community enjoyed the completion of new ventures such as the opening of the first 31 miles of the Leeds–Liverpool Canal from Liverpool to Wigan on 19 October 1774:

At 9 am the proprietors sailed up the canal in their barge, preceded by another filled with music, with colours flying and returned to Liverpool about one. They were saluted with two royal salutes of 21 guns each, besides the swivels on board the boats, and welcomed with the repeated shouts of the numerous crowds assembled on the banks. (T. Baines, *History of the Commerce and Town of Liverpool*, 1852)

A cold collation was served to the proprietors on the quay, and in the evening there was a dinner at George's Coffee House. A dinner was also given to the 215 workmen (mainly navvies) who had built the canal. Apart from its important goods traffic, the company provided a packet boat service at a penny a mile, which was used by many, including those going to the races on Crosby Marshes.

This passenger service may also have been used by members of the exclusive merchant dining club, the Mock Corporation of Sephton, which dined in winter at Bootle and in summer at Sefton. After a Sunday sermon the members regaled themselves in style at the local inn. There was a drinking test before admission to membership, and quantities of wine were wagered on cocks and horses. Some found it all too much. One Sunday in November 1788, as the club secretary recorded, Burgess Dunn, on his way home after dinner, 'involuntarily, but yet of his own accord and without any impulse *ab extra*, walked into the Canal, where he was exposed to a most copious ablution'.

For most of Liverpool's population in the second half of the eighteenth century, life was very different. The majority were un-skilled, employed in casual jobs at the docks. As a result they were low-paid and frequently out of work. In 1771 there were 6,000 common seamen in Liverpool, ready prey for the press-gangs working to swell the ranks of the Royal Navy. Being a seaport, many wives and mothers waited anxiously, and all too often in vain, for their men to return from a voyage in order to feed the family. The streets were full of disabled seamen and beggars, Irish labourers and seasonal migrants from the countryside, travellers to Ireland and emigrants. Liverpool's housing was cramped and unhealthy. Many parts of the town, especially on the north side, were very low-lying. Something approaching a swamp had to be filled when Williamson Square was laid out for a market in 1764. From the 1780s many of the poorer inhabitants were having to live in cellars originally intended for storing merchandise, or in courts squeezed in behind the elegant street-fronts admired by Defoe. Epidemics occurred frequently, and the public health problem grew steadily, finally reaching a crisis in the 1840s.

The growth of Liverpool in the eighteenth century was in no small measure connected with its success in the triangular trade between England, West Africa and the West Indies. Liverpool exported Manchester cottons, Birmingham ironwares and other goods to West

Africa, and imported West Indian sugar for home consumption or for re-export. The third side of the triangle, the 'Middle Passage' between West Africa and the West Indies gave the trade its notoriety. The cargo on this stretch was slaves, who were transported from the slave markets of West Africa to the sugar plantations of the West Indies — Spanish and French, as well as British.

Liverpool was associated with the slave trade for just over one hundred years. Although the British had been involved in the slave trade since John Hawkins's voyage in 1562, Liverpool's first slave ship (ironically named *The Blessing*) sailed in 1700. Thereafter Liverpool's share of the trade gradually increased. In 1730 15 slave ships were registered at Liverpool, and by 1751 there were 53. The most important period of growth was in the second half of the eighteenth century. In 1773 105 'slavers' sailed from Liverpool representing about a third of the total tonnage involved in the trade, and by 1795 Liverpool-registered ships were carrying over half the British slave traffic. The trade involved 100 of the town's principal merchants, as well as large numbers of seamen, and all the ancillary trades. G.F. Cooke, the alcoholic actor who had a reputation throughout the north, could with some justice exclaim that the very bricks of the town were cemented with African blood. From 1787 onwards, when the Committee for the Abolition of Slavery was formed, Liverpool found itself increasingly on the defensive against hostile criticism. The national campaign against slavery was led by William Wilberforce, whose father was a merchant of Hull, Liverpool's rival on the east coast. Local support was led by Dr James Currie, the physician at the Liverpool Dispensary and William Roscoe, a merchant and man of letters.

Liverpool merchants and slave captains regarded the criticism of Cooke and others as emotive and unreasonable. Liverpool only supplied a commodity needed in the West Indies. If they did not carry on the business other nations would, and Britain's wealth would pass elsewhere. As for the negroes, they were treated much better by English seamen than by their fellow Africans, and the hazards of the Middle Passage were shared by ship's crew and slaves alike. Liverpool's last slave captain, the one-eyed Hugh Crow, wished more attention were drawn to the evils of the press-gang and the conditions of 'white slaves'. The town was a business community. It did not have time to stop and consider the morality of its business transactions. The merchants were interested in the conditions of their slaves only insofar as they would make the transatlantic crossing without major damage to their value in the markets of the West Indies. The noble appeals of the abolitionists filled a moral vacuum.

The abolition of the slave trade by Act of Parliament in 1807 was a triumph for a new sense of the value of human life. It paved the way for the abolition of the press-gang and for parliamentary regulations of the treatment of children in factories and mines, and emigrants on ships, situations where, in the eighteenth century, efficiency was only tempered with humanity in individual cases.

While Liverpool was growing rich on its earnings from sugar, tobacco and slaves, a new industry was transforming large parts of south Lancashire. Cotton had been used to provide the weft in a variety of 'mixed' cloths since the mid-seventeenth century and Lancashire became famous for its fustians, a mixture of cotton and flax often used for linings of garments or underclothes. In the late seventeenth century the East India Company began to import from India, Persia and China large quantities of calicoes and muslins made exclusively of cotton. To help the English woollen industry, an Act of Parliament was passed in 1700 to stop the import of oriental printed fabrics, but they were so popular that plain calicoes continued to be imported, and printing works sprang up in London to meet the demand. Parliament tried to stop this by putting a heavy excise duty on these goods and, in 1720, prohibited the use or wear of any printed or dyed calicoes. The part of the Act dealing with goods which were a mixture of cotton and other materials was repealed in 1736, and there was considerable development of printing in Lancashire. One of the first printworks was Clayton's at Bamber Bridge, set up by 1759. In 1774 Parliament repealed the ban on English printed calicoes, although they were still subject to a heavy excise, and it was not until 1831 that all duties were finally removed.

Nevertheless, the Act of 1774 proved the signal for the great expansion of English cotton cloth production. Cotton quickly became immensely popular. As Macpherson wrote in his *Annals of Commerce* in 1785:

With the gentlemen, cotton stuffs for waistcoats have almost superseded woollen cloths, and silk stuffs, I believe, entirely: and they have the advantage, like the ladies' gowns of having a new and fresh appearance every time they are washed. Cotton stockings have also become very general for summer wear and have gained ground very much upon silk stockings, which are too thin for our climate, and too expensive for common wear for people of middling circumstances.

The competitiveness of the new cotton products was made possible by the inventions of Lancastrians like James Hargreaves, Richard Arkwright and Samuel Crompton who, encouraged by the expansion of weavers' output (thanks to Kay's flying shuttle), revolutionized the spinning process between 1765 and 1779. Hargreaves's 'jenny' multiplied the number of threads which could be spun on one machine; Arkwright's 'water frame' produced a strong enough thread for the warp of the cloth and could be adapted to water power; and Crompton's 'mule' allowed not only a strong thread, but also one fine enough to be woven into cloth for high-class muslins. Furthermore, the rapid introduction of Whitney cotton gins after 1793 enormously accelerated the cleaning of American raw cotton and greatly increased its availability.

Because of the demand for cotton cloth, and because of the invention of spinning frames and mules, capable of being harnessed to water power and too large to be accommodated in cottages, a number of mills sprang up alongside the becks which flowed off the Pennines. The mills were built by a variety of men — landowners, bankers, merchants — but they were rented and run by businessmen who became known as manufacturers or entrepreneurs. They took advantage of the defeat of Arkwright's attempts to defend his patent in 1785 and also of the boom in trade after the end of the War of American Independence in 1783. These entrepreneurs came from a variety of backgrounds. The first Robert Peel's father was a yeoman farmer; the father of John and Samuel Horrocks made millstones; nothing is known of Richard Arkwright's father, although Richard was first apprenticed to a barber. All these men ran cotton-spinning mills, often under great difficulties. Many went bankrupt or faded into obscurity. Others, like Arkwright and Peel, made enormous fortunes.

One entrepreneur about whom a good deal is known is Samuel Greg. Greg's father was a wealthy Belfast merchant and shipowner and two of his uncles were check and fustian manufacturers in Manchester. After an expensive education at Harrow and a grand tour of Europe, Samuel Greg settled down in Manchester to learn the secrets of the cloth trade at his uncles' King Street warehouse. There it was soon decided that he should take advantage of the developments in cotton-spinning and set up a mill near Manchester using water-driven spinning and carding machinery. The search for a suitable site led him to Styal, near Wilmslow, about ten miles from Manchester. He bought the land from the Earl of Warrington, and in 1784 erected a four-storey brick mill at a cost of £16,000. When his partner died the following year, Greg moved to Styal with his new wife, Hannah Lightbody, the daughter of a Liverpool merchant.

Meanwhile at Caton, near Lancaster, Hannah's sister Elizabeth was helping her husband, Thomas Hodgson, to set up another water-powered cotton mill to take advantage of the revival in trade following the signing of peace with the Americans at Paris in 1783. Thomas and his brother John had been born in Caton, of farming stock, and had gone to Liverpool to make their fortunes.

Caton was situated four miles from Lancaster, a flourishing port in the 1780s with a new dock under construction at Glasson, and with turnpike roads to Kendal and Preston. It was not therefore as remote from the Hodgsons' Liverpool business as might at first be thought. A domestic weaving tradition and plentiful woodland, ideal for bobbins and machine-making, may have reassured the Hodgsons in their choice. Above all, as their Greg relatives had found at Styal, the Hodgsons at Caton were assured of a constant supply of fast-flowing soft water. The site chosen was a corn mill where the Artle Beck descended to the water-meadows which flanked the river Lune. The Artle Beck provided a reliable source of power, not only for the Hodgsons, but also, by 1800, for three other mills. It is not surprising therefore that water rights were carefully defined in the leases and that they could be the cause of heated arguments among the mill-owners. The Hodgsons built another mill nearby and leased it out in 1788 to a Lancaster silk merchant named James Noble. As opportunities expanded, the Hodgsons built a third mill, Willow Mill, and converted a former forge into another cotton mill.

Their first mill, the four-storey Low Mill, remained the Hodgsons' largest. There is no record of what machinery it contained when it was first built in 1783, but a sale notice of 1814 from the *Lancaster Gazette* tells us that by then it contained the following:

The machinery consists of a Batting-machine, a Blowing ditto, 56 Carding-engines, 7 Drawing and Roving-frames, 4 Stretching-frames, 366 Spindles, 38 Water Spinning-frames and 4 Throstle ditto, 2684 Spindles, Winding and Warping-mills and all other articles necessary for carrying on the business to the best advantage;

2 Water-wheels, and a Steam-engine of 10 horses power by Boulton and Watt. The Stream of Water is powerful, the fall now used nearly 40 feet, and capable of being considerably increased.

The list shows that by 1814 there was a steam engine to provide power in case the water supply dried up. The Hodgsons' work force, judging by other mills, was probably two-thirds children under 18 and the rest women, with a few men in their twenties. The main jobs of carding and spinning were done by the adult women. Children helped by keeping the machines continually clean and by tying the broken threads. Their size enabled them to get underneath, and their small fingers were ideal for tying the fine threads. There were a few jobs for men as over-lookers, timekeepers, warehousemen and general labourers.

In the 1780s one machine was still small enough to be operated by a single family. Family work was what many domestic workers were used to, and to engage whole families made the mill-owner's job of recruitment simpler and the enforcement of punctuality and discipline easier. On the other hand, country villages like Caton presented grave labour difficulties for the entrepreneur. They had small populations, primarily concerned with agriculture and available only for part-time domestic employment as spinners or weavers. Younger sons and daughters of farmers may well have provided the first recruits for the Hodgson or Greg mills, but they could not supply the whole need. Parish authorities in London and Liverpool and in overpopulated rural areas of the south and east wrote to the mill-owners offering to send them poor families who would be glad of employment at their mills. Greg made special provision for new families by converting farm buildings into cottages, and after 1790 he erected brick terraces equipped with cellars for use as loom-shops. At Caton, by 1804, there were eight cottages attached to Low Mill and 25 at Willow Mill, all presumably built by the Hodgsons. In some places workers clubbed together to build their own cottages. At Longridge a building society was formed in 1793 with 19 subscribers. By 1802 13 houses had been built each 'with Necessary and Coalhouse'.

Pauper families provided some of the children needed to work the early mills, but most mill-children were pauper orphans. They were bound by indenture, like ordinary apprentices, to serve their master for seven years in exchange for clothing, board and lodging, but, unlike craft apprentices, factory apprentices could not expect a trade or permanent livelihood at the end of the apprenticeship. They were taken from their parish of birth and often carted tens or even hundreds of miles to factories like Low Mill. A few came from the neighbourhood. In 1819 a workhouse was established at Caton, under Gilbert's Act of 1782, for the poor of Caton and adjacent Lunesdale parishes. Some children from this workhouse worked in the Hodgson mills. Their pay, amounting to 8d (3½p) a week each, was given to the workhouse.

At Styal, Samuel Greg at first boarded his parish apprentices with farmers and then built a special house for them. The Hodgsons at Caton did the same. They converted what had formerly been the miller's house. Later, as their works grew, they built an extension to the house to provide accommodation for up to 100 children between the ages of nine and sixteen. From this house they probably supplied all their Caton mills. The apprentices' accommodation comprised separate eating-rooms and dormitories for the girls and boys. There were also a kitchen, wash-house and bake-house. While in the apprentice house the children were under the strict supervision of a master and mistress, but Sunday was the only day of the week that they were there for long.

Up at 4.30 am, the apprentices had to be at work by 5.00 am and they were not back until 7.00 pm except for meal breaks. They were worked very hard, but were quite well fed by the standards of the time: at breakfast and supper they had milk, porridge and bread called riddle-bread or oatcake. Their daily dinner menu was: Sunday — meat and potato pie; Monday — broth, beef and cabbage; Tuesday — lobscouse (meat and potatoes); Wednesday — rice pudding; Thursday — lobscouse; Friday — salt-herrings and potatoes; Saturday — potatoes and onions. The Hodgsons leased over 11 acres of land on which they kept six cows and grew potatoes. Milk and potatoes were staples of the diet of most working people in the early nineteenth century, but there is no doubt that the Hodgsons provided their apprentices with fresher and cleaner milk than they could ever have received in the centre of Liverpool. If they were ill a doctor was called. The cost of keeping an apprentice was estimated at 5s 6d (27½p) a week in 1808, a great deal more than the cost of wages to a free child.

Treatment of apprentices varied enormously from mill to mill. At the worst they were over-worked, underfed, beaten excessively

111

and forced to live in squalor and rags. Backbarrow, near Ulverston, had a bad reputation for cruelty and typhus fever resulting from bad conditions. At the best, the apprentices were treated as well as at Styal, where Samuel Greg insisted on no more than two to a bed and new clothes every two years. At the better mills they were marched to church on Sundays, usually in special Sunday dress — though rarely as resplendent as Watson's apprentices from Penwortham Factory (at Middleforth) who attended Walton-le-Dale Church in brown coats with yellow collars and cuffs. At Caton special galleries were erected in the church for Hodgsons' apprentices. That they were reasonably dressed may be assumed from the tailors' and shoe-makers' shops attached to the mill. Sunday School was provided on Sunday afternoons, and on Sunday evenings the local schoolmaster read prayers and a short sermon in the apprentice house, a service to which the adult mill-hands also came.

In 1802 Parliament passed an Act 'for the Preservation of the Health and Morals of Apprentices and Others employed in Cotton and other Mills'. This Act was sponsored by Sir Robert Peel, father of the Prime Minister, and himself an employer of children in his cotton mills at Bury and Blackburn. Peel's aim was to make the conditions in good mills compulsory in all. One clause provided for the apprentices to be withdrawn from the mill for two hours a day to attend school. As the Act made no adequate provision for inspection it was largely ignored. At Caton, however, R.W. Dickson reported in 1808 that 'a schoolmaster is kept for the daily instruction of the apprentices'. Kitty Wilkinson, founder of the Liverpool Public Washhouse, was Low Mill's most illustrious apprentice. In her memoirs she recalled that there was a library and a playground. The results were good. When a House of Commons Select Committee looked into the educational provisions of the Act in 1816, they found that 62 out of the 68 children under 18 years employed as apprentices by Hodgson attended school, and that the 64 aged over 10 years could all read. These were better results than those of the Gregs' school at Styal, although there the Gregs had three times as many children to cope with.

By the standards of the time, including those of most boarding-schools, the Hodgson children were well treated. Kitty Wilkinson, looking back at her time at Low Mill, described it as 'heaven on earth'. Not all the apprentices were so happy, and a number tried to run away. Advertisements appeared in Lancashire newspapers to

112

try to catch the runaways, for whom the penalty might be six months in Preston House of Correction. All mill-work was dangerous before the fencing of machinery and tragedies occurred, even in the best mills. One victim was Edward Whitfield, a 15-year-old apprentice at Low Mill who got caught in the machinery and was mangled to death in April 1816.

The adults worked as hard as the apprentices, but unlike the apprentices they were paid for their labour. In 1790 a male factory operative could expect 10s (50p) to 12s (60p) a week, his wife 5s (25p) and his children 9d (4p) to 1s 6d (7½p). Together the family earned more than most families at that time. Their hours, however, were very long: a six-day, 72-hour week was the minimum, except if the mill was on short time or if a drought or unusually severe frost had put the water wheel out of action. There were two breaks for meals in that 12-hour day, and in 'the good time', children might be worked in shifts to keep the mill running for as long as 20 hours a day.

Many men had to find work outside the mill as weavers, craftsmen or labourers. As weavers they had much more freedom than their wives and children employed in the mills. Weaving did not become a factory job until after 1815. John Greg introduced power weaving at Caton in 1824, but at Styal power looms were only installed after Samuel Greg's death in 1834. Most cotton-spinning mills, whether in town or country, had acquired power-loom sheds by the 1830s.

The proximity of the countryside was one advantage of the mill villages, although enclosure was limiting popular use of the commons, and vigilant gamekeepers were on the look-out for anyone poaching rabbits, game or fish. The maximum penalty for poaching was death until 1828. Rural sports such as dog-racing and coursing were popular.

Celebrations of national events, such as the King's recovery from an acute attack of porphyria in 1789 or the peace of 1815, often followed the pattern of surrounding agricultural villages, with processions, races and dancing, and plenty of bread, cheese and ale. Some or all the festivities would be provided by the master, but it was his concern to make such holidays as infrequent as possible because of the difficulty of getting his men back to work in a sober state afterwards. At Dolphinholme, in Wyresdale, on St Blaize's day (the festival of wool-combers) the workers processed the seven miles into Lancaster preceded by 'a band of musick', paraded outside the home of their employer, William Hinde, ate a hearty dinner at one of the Lancaster inns, drank innumerable loyal toasts and then staggered home.

The mill villages lacked the amenities of the towns, although every effort was made to make up for this. Dolphinholme claims to have been the first place to have been lit by gas which was introduced to light the mill in 1799. Shopping was more difficult. The Hodgsons at Caton ran a grocer's shop attached to Willow Mill, and there were probably other village shops as well, but village prices were usually higher than in town and there was less choice. The factory shop was known as the truck shop, and, at Styal, payment was by weekly account deducted from wages. Truck shops were identified in the popular mind with adulterated food, short measure and insolence, as portrayed by Disraeli in *Sybil*. Parliamentary reports suggest that the worst truck shops were in mining areas. Some cotton districts such as Chorley and Ramsbottom were also bad as the Select Committee on the Payment of Wages found in 1842.

Every mill village had its public house. Caton had several. Public houses were regarded by magistrates as places of violence and vice, but, as in towns, they performed a variety of essential functions. Apart from being the ideal place for refreshment and relaxation and often the venue of cockfights (until prohibited by law in 1834), the pub was about the only place for benefit club or friendly society to meet, or for local business, such as property sales, to be transacted. Large meetings occasionally proved too much even for a newly built pub, as at Hyde, in 1829, when the Norfolk Arms collapsed under the weight of a cotton spinners' meeting and 30 people were killed. The only alternative venues were the mill or one of the chapels built by the mill-owner or his employees. The Hodgsons allowed Independent preachers to use the mill-buildings for their meetings. It was not until 1829 that an Independent chapel was built at Caton. The Methodists held their first meetings at the Ship Inn, later in a barn, and finally, in 1836, in their own chapel, built with the help of a Methodist mill-manager. Roman Catholics had to walk to Hornby or Lancaster. Some mill-owners made special provision for non-sectarian meetings. Sir Thomas Bazley at Barrow Bridge, near Bolton, provided a large institute for his workers which Prince Albert visited in 1851. At Lostock Hall, near Preston, the mill-owners provided a library and a museum.

The worst aspect of such a community was the dependence of the people for work on one employer. This tension must have been increased when he, too, lived in the village. It was better at Caton where the Hodgsons, when not in Liverpool, lived at Escowbeck on the edge of the village. At Dolphinholme one of the partners lived next to the mill on the village street. In such conditions, trade unions were virtually impossible — even after the repeal of the Combination Acts in 1824-5. The old mediaeval adage of 'town air makes free' still applied in a metaphorical sense. Some attempts at forming unions were made. There was a strike at Dolphinholme in 1832 against a reduction in wages, but it was soon broken by the employers bringing in 'black-sheep' labour from the surrounding farms. At Caton the most the Gregs had to cope with was the occasional 'riotous assembly' and more frequent petty crimes, such as burglary and poaching.

Mill villages became out-dated when the general application of steam power to textile processes made it possible to build mills in towns, where, if land was more expensive, some amenities already existed and the labour supply was more flexible. In Lancashire, cotton manufacture became concentrated on the coalfields, even if canals and railways allowed the continued operation of mills in towns more distant from coal such as Preston or Lancaster. After the Napoleonic Wars profit margins narrowed as foreign competition increased. The era of enormous fortunes made by entrepreneurs such as Sir Richard Arkwright was over. The peace brought dislocation and depression. The Fieldings, who ran a country mill at Catterall, near Garstang, which had sent cotton goods as far afield as Peru in 1815, were bankrupt by 1830. The Hodgsons at Caton also had financial difficulties. In 1804 they had disposed of Willow and Forge Mills and had been obliged to mortgage the Escowbeck estate to their Lancaster and Manchester creditors. But it was more probably old age and lack of inclination to mill-work in their sons which made them sell Low Mill as well in 1814 — to their south Lancashire relative, Samuel Greg.

Samuel Greg replaced the steam engine at Low Mill, built a school for the apprentices and local children and built more cottages for the workers. He sent his second son John to supervise the Caton and Lancaster mills, while his three other sons looked after those at Styal, Bollington and Bury. The Bollington and Bury mills were sold in 1848, but the Caton and Lancaster mills remained under

Greg ownership until the Cotton Famine, during the American Civil War. John Greg continued to reside at Escowbeck, but as squire rather than employer. Low Mill continued to produce cotton warp until the 1970s, one of the longest surviving of Lancashire's late eighteenth-century country cotton mills.

Lancashire was full of growing communities at the end of the eighteenth century. Caton, like many others, had a mixed economy with families drawing their livelihood from both industry and agriculture. Hand-loom weaving dominated many villages, especially south of the Ribble. Life in Caton has been described from the mill-worker's point of view; the neighbouring community of Wyresdale gives a typical example of a farmer's life. Here, too, there was a cotton mill (at Catshaw) and a sizeable weaving element (at Tarnbrook), but as at Caton and elsewhere in Lancashire in this period, many families relied entirely on agriculture for a living.

One upland farming family was that of Cragg. Seventeenth-century farm buildings in Wyresdale bear their initials, although they were probably farming in the district much earlier. We are fortunate that in the late eighteenth century one of the family, David Cragg (1769-1835), was an assiduous diarist. The family farm was at Greenbank in Wyresdale, although David farmed others at different times. They were all small dairy farmers, mainly producing butter and cheese for the Lancaster market. Sheep and geese were kept as well as cattle, and a little oats was grown. Surplus oatmeal was sold at Lancaster or Preston markets, and any extra cattle were sent to the nearby cattle fairs at Marshaw, Cockerham or Lancaster. Cragg described a visit on 24 March 1789: 'We took two beasts to Cockerham fair and sold them for £16 0s 0d. It was a moderate fair: the beasts sold low and not many sold either. There was at the fair 98 beasts, which is reckoned a deal for that fair.' These small fairs disappeared in the course of the nineteenth century when the railways opened up more distant markets.

The major business trip of the year was to the Lancaster cheese fair in October. Bad weather, as in 1791, could make it a difficult and unpleasant day:

In the morning we got up intending to set off to Lancaster with the cheese at two o'clock, but it rained so very fast that we were weather stayed till four, and then the rain moderated, but rained some all the way to Lancaster. We saw no cheese carts till we got to Galgate, and we met five or six going to the Fair, and we

116

got before them going up the Long Lane brow. We got to Lancaster before seven o'clock, the road very mucky. We got pretty readily into the market, but when we had done unloading we had like not to have got back again. We stayed a long time before we could stir, but at length we got out. There was a great deal of cheese, and sold from 33s to 43s a cwt. Ours sold for 42s and we had 17 cwts 1 qr 26lbs. Cheese fell towards the latter end of the day. It was a very dirty fair raining all day till six o'clock at night.

Private sales of sheep, horses and cattle also took place. To encourage potential buyers, some laid on food and drink, but Cragg remarked sourly of one sale that it was 'very dear sale *and nothing to drink*'. Beer was an important element in the diet, although drinking to excess or idling in alehouses was disapproved of in what since George Fox's preaching in the 1650s had been a largely Quaker district. Total abstinence, however, did not become a feature of Wyresdale farming life until the mid-nineteenth century.

Labour on the farm was provided by the family and a few farm servants. David Cragg had four brothers and three sisters. Like his parents, he too had eight children. A small farm could not support all these, even if there were jobs for the men in ploughing, harrowing, shearing, hay-making and walling, and for the women in milking and making butter and cheese, apart from looking after the house. Marriage was the signal for a man to break away and rent his own farm, but he had to save up a long time for this moment. Farm servants did the rounds of the farms, changing twice a year at the hiring fairs at Whitsun and Martinmas. Large farms might have several servants. They lived in and received full board until they had saved up enough from their pocket money to get married and rent a cottage.

The two great ages for building farmhouses in Lancashire were 1680-1740 and 1840-1870. Eighteenth-century farmhouses rarely showed strong classical influence, although symmetry was more apparent than earlier. Fireplaces at either end of the house were one sign of the changing times, although windows were often still mullioned and the only external adornment was the porch. Some houses had a cellar for salting bacon and cheese, in addition to the standard two storeys.

David Cragg's first married home was smaller than the usual farmhouse, with only two rooms upstairs and two down. Downstairs were the parlour and buttery 'and a place under the stairs for the coals, as a cellar &c'. Outside was a small garden and a stable with two stalls, one of which he used as a 'shop' for the dog, the other as a turf house.

Turf or peat was the main fuel in Wyresdale, before the Lancaster canal brought coal. Some summers were so wet, however, that no turf could be got and there was a 'famine of fire'. Under such circumstances the Craggs took carts to the nearest available coal supply, whether at Smear Hall near Wray, or Preston, or even as far as Standish. Lime to improve the pastures had to be fetched from Kellet or from Sykes in the Trough of Bowland. Such expeditions took all day, for even the turnpike roads were very bad. Many of the by-roads were not even turnpiked and only rudimentarily maintained by local farmers such as themselves. Cragg was a great walker and left fascinating accounts of his walks to Ackworth School and Carlisle. For the walker at the turn of the nineteenth century the surface of the roads was less of a problem than the lack of signposts, and, as always, 'starkness' or stiffness of the limbs.

David Cragg had been taught to read and write at the age of 11 along with his sister Margaret, by a Master Goff at Shireshead Chapel. As he grew older he built up a little library of books purchased at Preston or Lancaster on market days. He did his own bookbinding, wrote jingles in his diary, and began a statistical account of Wyresdale. This was never finished, but the diaries are full of little cameos of local life. He describes the surveyors deciding on the line for the Lancaster Canal, and he mentions a trip on one of the first packet boats from Galgate to Lancaster. He saw some of the first ships to sail from Glasson Dock (completed in 1787) and watched a launching from the old shipyard on the Lune.

Occasionally he mentions civic and political life. The borough of Lancaster included part of the old forest of Quernmore and, in May 1788, young David watched the Mayor and Corporation on one of the periodic boundary-ridings: 'there was 43 horsemen and three or four footmen, they had three colours, and a drum and fife, a bassoon, a hautboy and a French horn'. The chief landowner in Wyresdale was J.F. Cawthorne of Wyreside Hall, notorious for embezzlement as colonel of the Middlesex militia, who represented the borough of Lancaster in several Parliaments. His keen guard against poachers made him unpopular, but the Wyresdale freemen, including the Craggs, voted for him in opposition to the Lowthers, a rich and powerful Cumbrian family who had established a strong interest in the borough by this time. Cragg, who described part of Cumbria, accurately, as 'the Lowther dominions', noted that in Lancaster at the 1796 election 'one man with a yellow riband in his hat went down the street shouting "Lowther, guinea, Lowther"'.

David Cragg was a member of the Society of Friends or Quakers like many of his neighbours. He attended Wyresdale meeting every Sunday, went to Lancaster for the monthly meeting, and occasionally to Carlisle or Preston for the quarterly meeting. Quaker rules on marriage nearly upset David's intentions, but fortunately his girl-friend, Molly Pye, became a Friend too, and they were married in 1807. One of their sons, Timothy, later spent a year at the Quaker school at Ackworth near Pontefract.

Financial troubles, a large family and dislike of his landlord made David Cragg restless after some years of married life. Emigration was one answer to a small farmer's problems in the early nineteenth century, and it suited David's temperament. His cousin Thomas emigrated to America in 1805, and his brother Timothy settled in Ohio in 1821. Twelve years later David, too, made the great decision. His wife Molly had died a few years earlier, and he and his eight children decided to make a new start. The cost of the passage on the *Six Sisters* from Wardleys on the river Wyre was £2 a head, with a further 10s (50p) to be paid to the government on reaching Quebec. He described his feelings as the ship sailed out of the estuary:

Wednesday April 3rd 1833. Set sail on board the Six Sisters from Wardleys in Old England, bound to Quebec in Canada . . . . 11 o'clock. A fine day, wind south. Shouting and hurrahing and waving of hats by those on board and answered by a great crowd on shore. Fired off the gun and away we went and bid adieu to Old England forever. So long William and all the hen-pecked club, the performing parliament, the tithes, taxes, church rates, parsons, and parasites, our friends and our enemies and our cursed land-lord, the calico pelican King of Misery at Lancaster.

The journey was not all plain sailing. Nine Craggs and their belong-ings shared an area only 12 ft (3.6 m) by 9ft (2.7 m) and 5½ ft (1.7 m) high. Cooking was done communally on deck. The voyage took 60 days, but the Craggs wrote home urging friends and relatives to join them in Upper Canada where there was plenty of work and good wages. Like many an emigrant, David Cragg never returned.

8 THE AGE
OF STEAM

The steam engine, as adapted by James Watt to power machinery in 1782, brought an end to the factory village phase of the Industrial Revolution. Steam engines proved much more reliable than water wheels although they were more costly to install and run. What they needed was a good supply of cheap coal. This was made possible by the canal system. Pioneered in 1761 by James Brindley and the Duke of Bridgewater between the Duke's mines at Worsley and the centre of Manchester, canals between towns in the Manchester area were dug in the 1790s, and east Lancashire towns received the benefit of the Leeds–Liverpool Canal in 1816.

Matthew Boulton the ironfounder and his partner James Watt held exclusive rights over their steam engine patent until 1800. Between 1785 and 1800 the Birmingham firm supplied 82 steam engines to the cotton trade, totalling 1,473 horsepower. Other firms soon began imitating them, even before their patent ran out. Nevertheless, the main investment in steam engines, as in power looms, took place after 1815. The number of cotton factories in Lancashire grew from 344 in 1819 to 1,815 in 1839. By this time the typical mill was the 'double' mill in which both spinning and weaving were carried on under one roof, so different from the days of Samuel Greg. The consumption of raw cotton grew from 7 million pounds (3,175,200 kg) weight in 1780 to 52 million (23,587,200 kg) in 1800. By 1831 it was 266 million (120, 657,600 kg) and by 1854, 764 million (346,550,400 kg). The export value of cotton cloth increased from £355,060 in 1780 to over £35 million by 1830.

The population leaped ahead, too. That of the county of Lancaster more than tripled between 1780 and 1830; in 1821 it had topped one million; by 1851 it was over two million; by 1881 it was more than three million. Much of the growth before 1800 had been of small communities but, as steam replaced water and muscle power, it was the growth of towns which was the most striking.

Towns were transformed. Liverpool and Manchester became the twin giants of the age. Each had a population of about 20,000 in 1760. By 1830 Liverpool's population was approaching 200,000 while Manchester and Salford between them were well over that figure. Other towns in the Manchester area and in east Lancashire also grew rapidly. The character of towns seemed to change with their growth. Preston, which Defoe had described in 1725 as a fine town uncharacterized by industry, full of lawyers, had 'no fewer than forty factories' by 1825. In Blackburn, where there was only half the number of factories of Preston, an inhabitant complained that 'although once very eminent for the wealth and respectability of its traders', these had mostly gone elsewhere, and the town had become 'almost wholly confined to the manufacturing of calicoes'. Certainly the social imbalance between rich and poor seemed greater with the increasing polarization of employer and employee, but the fine houses of Avenham in Preston and of Richmond Terrace in Blackburn gave the lie to the notion that early nineteenth-century mill towns were only occupied by the working class.

Our knowledge of the life of the cotton towns is enhanced by the observations of middle-class intellectuals like Mrs Gaskell and Friedrich Engels who lived in them, albeit somewhat reluctantly. Engels's work captures something of the desperation of life at the bottom of Manchester society, in the squalor of Ancoats or 'little Ireland'. Mrs Gaskell, who lived in Manchester for longer and who accepted the prevailing liberal ethic of its leaders, provides us with a more complete picture.

Born in Chelsea and brought up in Knutsford, Manchester was a shock to Elizabeth Gaskell, when she came to 14 Dover Street as the wife of the assistant Unitarian minister in 1832. The sheer size of the place was impressive — not so much in its physical area, but in the teeming numbers of people crammed into the courts and alleys which led off the main streets and surrounded the mills. In the heart of the town Mrs Gaskell felt far from the countryside in spirit, even though the distance in miles was not great. It was the noise and bustle that struck her, just as Margaret in *North and South* was amazed how: 'every van, every waggon and truck, bore cotton,

121

either in the raw shape in bags, or the woven shape in bales of calico'. Manchester had become the capital of the cotton cloth trade by the 1780s. In Mrs Gaskell's time it was one of the chief commercial centres of the world. Manufacturing caused heavy pollution of the atmosphere. Like London, Manchester quickly acquired a reputation for 'thick yellow' November fogs which seemed to enter everything and shut out all other life. Washing was a full-time occupation. As Mrs Hale complained to the mill-owner, Mr Thornton in *North and South*: 'I only know it is impossible to keep the muslin blinds clean here above a week together . . . . And as for hands — Margaret, how many times did you say you had washed your hands this morning before twelve o'clock? Three times, was it not?' The Hales were lucky to have water to wash with. Most Mancunians were too busy to spare time for washing more than once a day, and then only perhaps face and hands. Water was only laid on to wealthier homes; everyone else had to fetch from the pump or buy from the water-carrier.

Yet in many ways Mrs Gaskell loved what she called 'dear old dull ugly smoky grim grey Manchester'. She saw its advantages to the people. The bustle and speed of town life prevented the 'stagnant habits' of country people. There was an independence about the working Mancunian which was denied to rural labourers or workers in a mill village. Wages were steady in rural areas, but at 'starvation' level, whereas in Manchester and the cotton towns, workers were better paid. Families employed in cotton manufacture could afford butcher's meat on Sundays 'in the good time' and could afford to furnish their homes decently, with money even for a clock and a few ornaments. Alternatively something could be spared for the sick club or burial society and for the children's education at Sunday school.

It was undoubtedly a hard life when the mills were shut down by depression, as happened too often in the years 1837-48. Slack trade caused bankruptcy among mill-owners and tradesmen and unemployment among factory workers and labourers. In such times the potential grimness of Manchester life became reality. No money for coal meant cellar and court dwellers suffered the full consequences of their damp and unwholesome environment. Furniture and even clothes went to the pawnshop. Poverty might necessitate a 'flit' to some cheaper accommodation in a more crowded and desperate part of town. The only food that could be afforded at such times was a slice of bread and cheese and a little old tea. In such reduced circumstances young children died of 'famine' fever (typhus), while elder brothers and sisters were sucked into the twilight world of pickpockets and prostitutes. Parents became sullen and listless. Workers' clubs and unions ran out of money too and strikes were of little help. All that could be hoped for was an improvement in trade.

Engels described the casual labourers of Ancoats; Mrs Gaskell the cotton workers in prosperity and poverty. Life could be equally hard for even those on the fringes of 'respectable' employment. The days of clerks and shopworkers were as long and arduous in many respects as those of the manual workers. Keen competition between shops in the same town meant that they remained open for very long hours. Not all an assistant's time, however, was spent behind the counter. It was not until the late nineteenth century that the retailer became largely concerned with the sale of pre-packaged goods. Before then there was much preparation to be done by assistants and apprentices behind, above, or even underneath the shop.

A vivid account of such work was given by Edward Frankland, apprentice to a Lancaster chemist and grocer in the 1840s. His day began at 5.45 am (an hour later in winter), when he had to open up the shop. As junior apprentice he spent most of the day down in the cellar pounding drugs with a twenty-pound pestle. When pounding certain drugs he had to wear a linen bag over his head to protect himself from poisonous dust. This bag had to be taken off from time to time to prevent suffocation, but if he stopped pounding for long the chemist came clattering down the steps to find out why he was not working. Frankland had an hour for dinner, except on Saturdays when the shop was so busy that dinner was brought in by the chemist's wife. The shop did not close until 8.30 pm — an hour later on Saturdays. Many shops opened on Sundays as well. Later in his apprenticeship Frankland was given a week's holiday each year and promoted to pulling teeth. Later still he became Professor of Chemistry at Manchester and then London, but the memory of his early days in the chemist's shop haunted his dreams two or three times a week for the rest of his life.

Town life in Lancashire in the Industrial Revolution was not all drudgery. Somehow — often late on Saturday evenings — the towns-people found time to enjoy themselves. The calendar was full of local fairs for cattle, sheep, horses, cheese and pedlary, some of which have survived into the twentieth century. These, like Manchester's Knott Mill fair, attracted large crowds. Apart from the large range of goods for sale, there were travelling circuses — with wild animals and 'marvels' such as children with two heads — and traditional sports such as the baiting of bears, badgers and bulls, clog and cock-fighting and pugilism. Many such sports were brutal to our way of thinking, but the keen appetite for horror was also reflected in the lurid newspaper descriptions of the victims of fires and unfenced factory machinery. A crowd of 8,000 turned out, in 1857, to watch one of the last public hangings in Lancaster, and was very disappointed when the burial was delayed until late at night.

A new moral climate, however, was gradually emerging in the first half of the nineteenth century. The Evangelical Revival gave additional support to the demands of the propertied classes for a stronger moral discipline in a society undergoing rapid social change without an adequate police force. Acts of Parliament in the 1830s prohibited traditional sports such as cock-fighting and bear-baiting, at the same time as the New Poor Law was introduced and a more efficient police force was provided. Horse-racing and fairs ceased to be patronized by the 'respectable' classes, and were terminated by the magistrates because of their association with brawling, drunkenness and crime. Fairs continued longer in rural areas where they were justified by the shortage of shops. Banned sports such as cock-fighting lingered on in secret, and pitch and toss players — mainly teen-age boys — were frequently dragged before the police courts.

Traditional festivities, such as rush-bearing, also came under suspicion for the drinking and 'bloody noses' which accompanied them. The original purpose of rush-bearing — to provide a warm, dry floor covering in church — was no longer valid as churches were restored and refloored. However, the competition between small communities in decorating rush-carts, flying banners and organizing morris-dancers and 'bands of music' was such a colourful exercise, that it was hardly in decline before there were attempts at revival by folklorists and others. Hence in 1868 the lord of the manor of Rochdale tried to revive the tradition there by offering a prize of 10 guineas for the best rush-cart. His efforts were only temporarily successful. May Day survived better in many places, with may-poles, the dressing of horses and carts, may songs, and a may queen.

On the whole such communal rejoicings, especially in the bigger towns, were replaced by recreation along class lines. The more prosperous, along with the more earnest, turned to literary, scientific and artistic pursuits in the form of lectures at the Mechanics Institutes and kindred institutions. Shorter hours and free Saturday afternoons from the 1850s and 1860s — at least for mill workers — enabled teenagers and adults who had never been to day school to acquire a degree of literacy and perhaps some rudimentary technical knowledge. The huge expansion of the local newspaper press is one sign of their success. The less prosperous and less earnest turned to the bright lights of the beerhouse 'free and easy' and later the music hall. The coming of the railways offered opportunities for day excursions, for temperance and Sunday School treats and works outings. The greater popularity of public houses than churches or chapels at Blackpool, Southport and Morecambe became the subject for many a moral diatribe. Running races for prizes, such as a shoulder of mutton, were popular with men and boys alike. Pigeon-fancying, horse-racing and dog-racing continued to be favourites. Meanwhile, cricket and rowing grew in popularity with the middle classes, and at Lancaster there was an exclusive archery club called John o' Gaunt's Bowmen.

The Industrial Revolution created great wealth in Lancashire. This wealth may be seen partly in the vast increase of population and partly in the rapid growth of every type of industry. In terms of income there was great inequality. It was apparent to all in the differing lifestyles of factory owners and managers and their employees. In 1818 one journeyman cotton spinner indignantly described the employers as a set of men who made up for their lack of education with 'a display of elegant mansions, equipage, liveries, parks, hunters, hounds etc. sending their children to the most costly schools, 'petty monarchs . . . in their own particular districts'. Mrs Gaskell noted the contrast between the families of rich and poor during a trade depression: 'Carriages still roll along the streets, concerts are still crowded by subscribers, the shops for expensive luxuries still find daily customers, while the workman loiters away his unemployed time in watching these things . . . . ' (*Mary Barton* 1848).

This contrast between the indolent rich employer and his starving employee has often been pointed out. It is worth remembering however, that the first generation manufacturers themselves worked extraordinarily long hours and bore great financial risks. In spite of the very low level of taxation many failed and sank back to, or below, the level from which they had come. Many of the successful

125

encouraged their children in charitable and political work to improve the lot of the poor. That they did not change the system which had made their money is not surprising. The fact that Robert Owen exhausted a large fortune attempting to fulfil socialist dreams convinced most men of property that their scepticism about his cooperative ventures had been entirely justified.

The lives of many mill-owners do not bear out the level of luxury and irresponsibility so frequently suggested. Considering their wealth, many of their homes, although far better than those of their employees, often appear small and rather unimpressive in comparison with the homes of the landed gentry. The Horrocks homes at Lark Hill, Preston and Penwortham Lodge, built in the Napoleonic period, although solid and quite large, scarcely indicate that the family was one of the most successful of the age. John Horrocks, in ten years, built 5 mills and died at 36 in 1804, leaving £750,000. Yet it must be remembered that, in traditional English style, such men as John Horrocks and his brother Samuel were more concerned to maintain profits at their Stanley Street mills and to leave money for their families than to squander their fortune in architectural display, even though both brothers in turn had to cut a dash as a member of Parliament for Preston. Families who sold their businesses to buy land and upper-class status usually moved far from the neighbourhood of their mills. The Garnetts of Salford moved to Quernmore; the Peels moved to Warwickshire; the Horrockses simply died out.

In the first half of the nineteenth century manufacturing families, on the whole, remained closely attached to their businesses. Sometimes firms suffered because this emphasis on family ties failed to take sufficient account of differences in personality. The Greg brothers who looked after their father's mills did not have his gift or inclination. Friedrich Engels resented his work as general manager of his father's Manchester office, but had to carry out his duties for the financial rewards.

Many Manchester companies had London offices. At these, the sons of manufacturers often received part of their training. John Bury, son of a calico-printer of Pendle Hill and Manchester, was sent to the firm's London office in 1812 at the age of 23. There he learnt to supervise the receipt and delivery of stock, and the accounts made by clerks, who, seated at high desks, worked laboriously with quill pens and ledger. He had to read the financial press, see the firm's brokers, and keep a close watch on the state of the market. Close contact with overseas agents was necessary as it was important to provide them with sufficient stock but not flood them, because the state of the market could change very quickly. Back in Pendle there was the manufacturing side to look after and in Manchester the problems of packing and shipment, mainly through Liverpool.

The Burys had similar problems to countless other Manchester-based cotton firms. Bad trade might lead to inability to meet obligations and the suspension of business. In the days before limited liability individuals could be ruined overnight. Some took refuge in suicide. Friedrich Engels, who saw in each crisis the imminent collapse of capitalism for which he longed — in spite of the effects it would have on his own business — described the panic of 1857: 'Manchester is getting more and more deeply involved: the constant pressure on the market is having a terrific effect. Sales are impossible. Every day we hear of lower bids, and nobody with any self-respect tries to sell his goods any longer'. Yet the deliverance for which Engels looked never came, and the Manchester cotton market survived this and many other crises, before the capital of the world's cotton industry moved elsewhere in the twentieth century.

Manufacturing wealth had its advantages, even for Engels. How else would he have been able to support his friend, the struggling journalist, Karl Marx? How else would he have afforded to hunt with the gentry? Manufacturing wealth was spent in different ways by different manufacturers. Some, like Richard Cobden, went on prolonged foreign trips. He found the streets of Constantinople in February 'a thousand times worse than the Hanging Ditch or Deansgate in the middle of December'. Later, Cobden went into politics. During his career he was at different times member of Parliament for Stockport and Rochdale. He and his Rochdale friend, John Bright, became the foremost champions of free trade. Their success was marked by the repeal of the Corn Laws in 1846, and the memory of their cause and its importance to the Lancashire cotton industry was honoured by the erection of the Manchester Free Trade Hall. Other entrepreneurs spent their money on education, like John Owens, or on books and manuscripts, like John Rylands, or on pictures, like Lord Leverhulme. Many did not set their sights so high. For them a public school education for their sons, followed by university, marriage and a comfortable villa in a smart suburb, or later in Southport or St Annes, was all that they could safely afford.

The new-found wealth could be spent on land, houses, servants, books and holidays, but, in the first half of the nineteenth century at least, it could do little to relieve the suffering occasioned to all classes by ill-health. The Bury family papers provide illustration of this. During the Napoleonic Wars John Bury of Sabden paid several pounds a year to his doctor, Richard Hardy of Whalley, for medical visits and a variety of medicines. These palliatives included stomach linctus, alterative and cathartic powders, sedative mixture, expectorant pills, stimulating gargle, tonics and blistering sales and plasters. Some of these remedies were ineffective, some positively harmful. Dr Hardy made a number of visits to the Bury household every year, but even with all this attention, the Burys were not a healthy or long-lived family. One of the children had had what we now recognize as polio, and his father was on the constant look-out for a cure. In fact, of the nine children born between 1790 and 1807, only Charles, the polio victim, survived to his thirtieth year. The presence of death was as commonplace in middle-class families as in those of the working class.

Constant bereavements helped to reinforce the strong religious seriousness of many of the manufacturing and mercantile families. Much spare time was spent in such serious pursuits as charitable bazaars, literary evenings and later temperance meetings. John Bury wrote a religious poem on seeing the bier of a friend and later wrote little notes to himself as reminders of the need for spiritual strength in the hour of physical failure. Daily family prayers and church attendance on Sundays were the rule, but this did not prevent family amusements in the evenings. The Burys — who were Baptists — liked singing. At Liverpool, the Gladstones, equally serious Anglicans, all loved music too, and enjoyed dancing, cards and even the theatre.

Many middle-class pleasures became working-class pleasures too. Charles Hallé, who came to Manchester from Paris as a music teacher in 1848, replaced the exclusive Gentlemen's Concerts with an annual season of weekly public orchestral concerts in 1858. Such concerts were mainly attended by middle-class Mancunians, but their influence spread far and wide and Hallé's choice of music was echoed in many a chapel choir and glee club. Meanwhile an annual brass band competition was established at Bellevue. A rich and varied musical tradition is still a feature of north-western life.

Rail travel, too, was patronized mainly at first by the middle class, but its popularity quickly spread. Railway construction was characterized by hordes of drunken, godless navvies who frequently

15 Bearbaiting in Manchester. Animal-baiting, whether of bulls, badgers, dogs or bears, was popular in Lancashire as elsewhere until its suppression after 1835. This picture is based on an eighteenth-century print

16 Lancaster Old Bridge. Formerly a strategic point in the county's defences it was replaced by Skerton bridge in 1782 to accommodate a new quay in the heyday of the West Indies trade

17 Liverpool East Quay, Prince's Dock, 1833. This watercolour by Samuel Austin shows Lancashire's greatest port in the days before steam replaced sail. General cargo was handled at this dock, built in 1821

18 A hand-loom weaver at work. The golden age of this skill was the last quarter of the eighteenth century. Ephraim ('Owd') Eccles, pictured below *c.* 1909, was the last hand-loom weaver in Darwen

19 Factory-spinning, *c.* 1840. Although most spinners were women, here a male spinner is assisted by two piecers who tie the broken threads, while a young scavenger works underneath the mule

20 Farmer Jones. Jones is persuaded by Nan, the drunken pedlar, to buy her spoons, which are a safer investment than his corn and cheese. (Tim Bobbin, *Human Passions Delineated*, 1773)

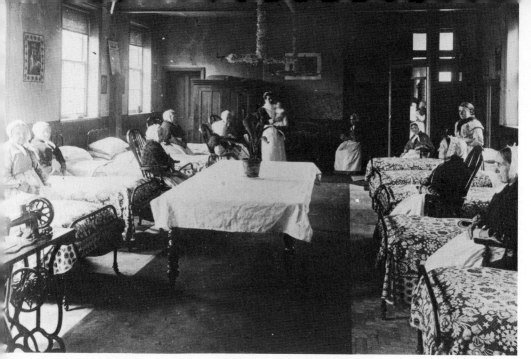

21 Interior of Oldham
Workhouse *c.* 1900.
Many old people who
had lost their relatives
spent their last years in
the union workhouse.
Discipline was strict,
and comforts were
intentionally minimal

22 The Knocker-up
c. 1900. This man
performed an essential
task in Burnley, as
others like him did in
every Lancashire
town in the days before
alarm clocks

23 Inside a Liverpool public house *c.* 1895. The 'nearest way out' of any town, pubs were constantly criticised by temperance reformers. Children were not banned by law from bars until 1908

24 Blackpool Beach, 1903. Note the wheel, once part of the Winter Gardens, erected in 1896 and dismantled in 1928, and the dining rooms which were in fierce competition with the boarding houses

25 Laying the foundation stone at Bury Grammar School, 1906. The ceremony is performed, with full masonic honours, by Lord Stanley (left), later 17th Earl of Derby, and Archdeacon Blackburne (right), Chairman of Governors

26 Bacup's Britannia Coconut Dancers. Originally migrant Cornish quarrymen, teams of 'Nutters', with blackened faces, costume and clogs, have danced with their 'coconuts' of polished wood through Bacup on Easter Saturday since 1857

27 Cockling in Morecambe Bay. One cockler brings the cockles to the surface by bouncing a 'jumbo' along the wet sand, while his companion uses a special fork or 'craam' to scoop them into her basket

28 The Lancashire contingent in the Jarrow March, 1936. Unemployment in Lancashire in the 1930s was higher than the national average, and many able-bodied unemployed joined the hunger marches to London

29 The Manchester Blitz, 1940. The morning after the night raid. The old streets are barely recognisable, but a wall poster still announces that 'Bette Davis (the filmstar) uses Lux soap'

30 Kirkby kids, 1979. Youngsters play football outside a row of shops in 'the only place in the world where the kids have to go out to play in three shifts'

broke off work to fight each other and terrorize the neighbourhood. But by the time the main rail network had been laid (*c.* 1845), writers were extolling the care with which railway companies treated their charges and the detail of the organization:

> The railway system is beautifully arranged, as far as regards the whole staff — there are the committee, secretaries, engineers, surveyors, station masters, engine drivers, stokers, pokers, guards, police superintendents, artificers, labourers, and waggoners or lurrymen. (P.A. Whittle, *Bolton-le-Moors*, 1855)

There were a number of accidents in the early days of the railways, the most spectacular of which was the death of William Huskisson, who as a former President of the Board of Trade had helped establish international agreements favourable to free trade in cotton. Huskisson fell in front of the Stephenson's 'Rocket' at the opening of the Liverpool and Manchester line at Parkside on 15 September 1830. Yet people were not put off. Stage coaches had carried 14,000 passengers a year between Liverpool and Manchester. By 1835 the railway was carrying half a million, not to mention the huge volume of freight. One attraction was speed: the journey to Liverpool now took under two hours. The other was economy: the fare was 7s (35p) first class and 4s (20p) second class. Railway companies were soon arranging third class fares for a penny a mile, and special excursion fares were to allow all but the poorest a day at the seaside at Blackpool, or even a trip to London to see the Great Exhibition of 1851.

Not everyone benefited from technological change. The hand-loom weavers, for example, who gained so much from the mechanization of spinning, suffered considerably when weaving in its turn became steam powered. This change occurred in bursts of industrial investment after 1815. The peace brought a short boom, followed by a long depression, but the number of cotton weavers continued to increase and piece-rates plummeted from at least 21s (£1.05) at the height of prosperity in 1802 to 8s 9d (44p) by 1817. Petitions to Parliament to institute a minimum wage were to no avail; the local differences as much as the Combination Acts prevented organized industrial action. In desperation after 1815, the weavers turned to demands for parliamentary reform. Reform societies, known as Hampden Clubs, after the opponent of Charles I, were formed in the villages round Manchester and a 'monster' meeting was held in

St Peter's Fields, in August 1819. It was broken up by the troops, leaving several hundred casualties and 11 killed. The hussars that had defeated Napoleon were now turned on the people in what became generally known as the 'Peterloo Massacre'.

The decline of the weavers' standard of living was made worse by depressions like that of 1826. A brief look at the conditions of north-east Lancashire, where 40% of the population were weavers will illustrate this. The depression created widespread bankruptcy and unemployment. Not all landlords could afford to follow the example of Lawrence Rawstorne of Penwortham near Preston who reduced the rent of all his hand-loom tenants by 10%. A Darwen weaver wrote to the *Blackburn Mail*: 'Ame weyvin for one on nane-pens a peece, an ave fore childer an me wife to keep into th' bargen, soe we monnod hev so monny flesh dinners.' Like the Bolton weavers, he and his family were probably existing on 'a solitary meal each day of oatmeal and water'.

By March 1826 with unemployment running at about two thirds of the population of the Blackburn area, there was a rash of robberies from grocers' shops and farms, and occasional outbreaks of violence. The house of the clerk to the justices was attacked by a mob armed with poles, and the passengers on the market coaches were bruised and cut by flying stones. To the relief of the men of property, the watchmen who, less than a year before, had been the laughing stock of the town after being found dead drunk in a midden on Blakely Moor, were now reinforced by a troop of Enniskillen dragoons. Their arrival did not, however, prevent a large crowd destroying power looms worth £12,000 at Accrington and Blackburn on 24 April. In the struggle between soldiers and rioters outside a mill in Grimshaw Park, one of the weavers was killed and several received fatal bullet-wounds.

In spite of fears of a general insurrection, the population was too weak for large-scale protest. When a doctor called to attend the birth of a weaver's child at Eanam, he found the child delivered, but already dead, alongside its mother lying half-dead from starvation on a heap of straw. The Blackburn workhouse was full to bursting. Local landowners distributed food and money and employed men in clearing woods, while the local relief committee distributed oatmeal, bacon, East India rice and treacle. Blankets were in desperately short supply, and vinegar had to be given to sufferers from typhus. Anglicans and Quakers (under Ann Ecroyd of Edgend near Burnley) worked hard to raise relief funds, and King George IV sent £1,000. Many Blackburn weavers decided to emigrate to the United States, but only a few could afford the passage, and they were warned that there were power looms there, too.

The minutes of the Select Committee of the House of Commons on the Handloom Weavers in 1834 give some idea of the financial plight and the injured pride of the weavers. Leading weavers, like John Lennon of Preston, resented having to send their children or wives to work in factories. They regretted their inability to provide for their children's education. They had no money left for membership of a sick club. When Lennon's wife fell ill he borrowed ten shillings from the agent at the Horrocks and Jackson warehouse in Preston. When James Brennan's wife was pregnant, all he could offer the midwife from the lying-in hospital was 'a little gruel and perhaps a gill of ale'. Lennon lived in a cellar with only a loomshop, bedroom and small kitchen. Brennan's weekly budget was probably fairly typical of a working man with a wife and two children at this time:

Soap: 1½d; 1lb Butter: 9d; 1½lb Sugar: 9d; 28lb Bread at 1½d: 3s 6d; 21lb Potatoes at ¼d: 5¾d; 7lb Oatmeat at 1s 2d for 10lb: 10d; 1½d worth milk per day: 10½d; ½lb Flesh Meat on Sunday: 3½d; Bacon: 1¼d; Coal: 10½d; Candles: 8d; Total: 9s 2½d.

His usual weekday dinner was buttermilk and potatoes. Candles, rather than some cheaper form of lighting, were necessary when mending breaks in the yarn. A further 4d (2p) a week went on two or three gills of 'malt liquor' on Saturday night.

Conditions improved little in the 1830s, although the overall number of weavers began to decline. Only after 1850, with the absorption of hand-loom weavers into other trades and with the general improvement in employment prospects did the work of such committees as Ann Ecroyd's become unnecessary.

After the disillusionment with the Whig Reform Act of 1832, which had given extra seats to the Lancashire towns but few extra votes, working-class grievances fround political expression in Chartism. Whig legislation, particularly the New Poor Law of 1834, aroused as much opposition as the Tory-sponsored Corn Laws of 1815. The Charter demanded universal suffrage, annual parliaments and payment of members, in order to introduce a popular element into the control of public affairs. It was, however, opposed by the new manufacturers as well as by the Whigs, and a middle-class rival was set up in the form of the Anti-Corn Law Association (later League).

The Chartist leaders hoped for a massive demonstration of popular support. In 1837-8 they held political lectures, open-air demonstrations and torchlight processions in the cotton towns. Local working-men's associations were formed to elect delegates to the Chartist National Convention, while the rank and file interrupted meetings of the Poor Law Guardians and those of the Anti-Corn Law League. By the summer of 1839 mass violence was feared. In Bolton a deputy constable was shown a box of 20 old files, marked with chalk and capable of being turned into pikes at ten minutes' notice — or so the Home Secretary was informed. Meanwhile the new county police force was being armed with sabres and horsepistols. At Bury a crowd attacked a detachment of police sent by train from London to help keep order.

When the Chartist petition was rejected by the House of Commons, the National Convention decided on a general strike to force the government's hand. A 'national holiday' or 'sacred month' was due to begin on 12 August, but at the last minute it was called off. In various Lancashire towns the great day had been preceded by nightly meetings and even demonstrations in the parish churches on Sundays. The national holiday was celebrated, in spite of the Convention, with turn-outs in many Lancashire towns. At Rochdale a crowd from Heywood was turned back by two local magistrates, Mr Ashworth in his gig and Mr Chadwick on foot, flanked by 60 soldiers. At Middleton the women cotton workers considered withdrawing their sick club money from the bank. At Bolton there were riots during which Little Bolton Town Hall was wrecked. Some places were quieter: at Blackburn the display of pikes and placards in the parish church had elicited no concessions from the vicar, Dr Whittaker, who urged his unusual congregation to attend more regularly and to avoid covetousness of other people's property. Blackburn Chartism was declared to have 'died of Dr Whittaker's sermon'; at Chorley, the Chartist cashier absconded with the funds.

In 1842, the year of the second Chartist petition, strikes once again reinforced political action. Further wage reductions in the fourth summer of depressed conditions sparked off strike protest in the towns of Ashton, Stalybridge and Dukinfield. The strikers pulled the plugs out of the boilers of the mill-engines and went from mill to mill, turning out their fellow workers. They marched into

Manchester, and from there engulfed virtually the whole of the cotton district, including such outlying places as Chorley and Preston. Crowds of turnouts, varying from a few hundred to over 10,000, moved from one town to another closing mills and pulling the plugs to keep them closed. On the whole, the police and the military behaved with restraint, but a clash between strikers and soldiers in Lune Street, Preston, led to the serious wounding of seven rioters, two of whom later died. The first strikes had taken place on 8 August. By the end of that month most of the Lancashire cotton workers were back at work at reduced rates. The authorities referred to the incident as the Plug Plot, but no evidence of a conspiracy has come to light.

In 1848 the Chartists presented their third and final petition, but in Lancashire support was somewhat muted by the depression and the lessons of previous years. There were a few demonstrations in the cotton towns and some support for Chartist candidates at elections, but as a united working-class political movement, Chartism was virtually dead.

The 1850s saw the revival of trade and the increase in popularity of trade unionism. The peaceful conduct of the Preston cotton strike of 1854 — in which the workers demanded, but failed to achieve a 10 per cent rise in wages — won respect and admiration for cotton workers all over the country. During the late 1850s and 1860s many unions developed, for skilled men like power-loom weavers and engineers, who could afford the high contributions. Such organizations also made an important contribution to the revival of political reform movements. These efforts were rewarded by the Second Reform Act of 1867 which gave the vote to working-class householders in the boroughs, and the Trade Union Act of 1871 which gave full legal protection to union funds.

Coal was the twin pillar, with cotton, of Lancashire's great expansion in the nineteenth century. The Romans seem to have been the first to use coal in the north-west, but it was not until the sixteenth and seventeenth centuries, when it was used for limeburning and salt production, that the industrial potential of coal began to be realized. The use of the steam engine in the cotton industry after 1790 was a major incentive for coal-mining in the nineteenth century. Coal was also used for glass-making at St Helens, as well as for domestic purposes. In the early nineteenth century the coalfield was exploited by a network of mining communities stretching from St

Helens in the south-west to Oldham in the east and Burnley in the north-east.

Mining was characterized by a large number of small pits, few of which were of any depth. Coal was owned by landowners, such as the Duke of Bridgewater, and dug up by a system of sub-contracting known as the butty system. Colliers were hired by the chartermaster or butty, and they in turn hired their own labour to bring the coal from the face to the surface. By this means it was easy for coal proprietors to claim complete ignorance of how the coal actually reached the surface. Only when the movement to abolish child labour got under way in the early 1840s did details of colliers' working arrangements become available to the general public.

The reports on children's employment in mines revealed that the colliers hired women and children to act as their 'drawers' — that is to drag or push the hewn coal from the face to the 'pit's eye' in smaller pits or the 'main-levels' in larger ones. The coal was carefully packed in tubs which were put on sleds or waggons. The children worked in teams, especially in the thinner 'mountain' seams where only the smallest could squeeze through. One was harnessed to the front to pull, and two were put on the back to push. In the larger seams a waggoner was in charge who might be as old as the getter or face worker. There might also be a 'jigger' whose job it was to jam on the brakes to slow the waggon as it reached the pit 'mouth'. Other jobs for children were the opening and closing of ventilation doors and the driving of pit-ponies at the pit-mouth. Commentators agreed that this last job was the 'most agreeable work in the mine'.

Boys and girls went down the pits at an early age. In the St Helens area they started work about the age of eight or nine, but where the seams of coal were thin, as in the Rochdale area, the services of four and five-year-olds were required. Boys and girls were treated alike. In many ways, girls were preferred as drawers to boys, for they were said to be steadier workers and less anxious than boys to become better-paid coal-getters. Only men from the age of 18 or so upwards worked at the coal-face. Women continued to act as drawers into their 20s and 30s and were invaluable in the larger seams. Many women carried on working even when they were pregnant. Mary Hardman of Outwood near Radcliffe gave her sobering evidence to the Commission of Inquiry of 1842: 'I have had either three or four children born the same day that I have been at work, and I have gone back to my work nine or ten days after I lay down almost

142

always. Four out of the eight were still-born'.

The work was long and arduous. Many pits worked round the clock, some on a two-shift, others on a three-shift system. The shortest working day in any pit was eight hours and might rise to 12 or 13 hours. Drawers often worked two hours longer to clear any back-log. The only meal-break was the half-hour or hour for dinner, consisting of bread and butter (butty) or bread and cheese.

Some witnesses before the Commission of 1842 made much of the 'family' nature of the work in the Lancashire pits. To prudish critics this helped to excuse the semi-nudity of the miners. Family ties did not preclude cruelty. One drawer remarked about her husband (a getter) that 'my fellow has beaten me many a time for not being ready'. Other getters took 'liberty with the drawers'. The world of the collier and his family was rough and brutalized. Colliers were not slow to strike their drawers with whatever was available, pick-arm, belt or foot. Nor did they distinguish much between lasses and lads. The pauper children who were 'apprenticed' to some colliers probably came off worst. The older boys quickly copied the habits of the adults, and one 10-year-old's rump was reduced to 'jelly' after 12 strokes with a 'cut' for bringing no dinner down the mine and supposedly stealing another's.

Accidents were so common that only the Duke of Bridgewater's mine bothered to record them. Ropes broke on the winding gear, and unsurfaced shafts shed rocks as chairs and baskets banged against the sides. Explosions of 'fire-damp' (carburetted hydrogen) were reputedly less common than in Newcastle, but they still took their toll. Cuts and grazes from walls and roofs or chains and belts were commonplace. Nystagmus permanently damaged miners' sight. Only at an enlightened pit like Chamber and Werneth of Oldham was there provision of free medical assistance, pit regulations on placards and lamps for the men's use. There was no cure for exhaustion except rest, and there was little chance of that.

The great attraction of mine work was the high pay. At Oldham the colliers earned 5s (25p) a day, while waggoners earned 3s (15p) and the children 7d (3p). Even the Duke of Bridgewater's men, although underpaid at 14s (70p) to 16s (80p) a week, received a big concession in that their cottage and garden rent amounted to a maximum of £2 a year. Of course the system of payment by the fortnight, or even by the month, meant that the collier had to live off credit for much of the time, and prices at truck shops were

143

usually inflated, but come pay-day he was off to enjoy himself, as an underlooker at Ringley Bridge pointed out (again in 1842):

> . . . they are never expected to come on the Monday after pay; an *odd* man may come to keep the roads straight but that is all; and when they come on a Tuesday they are not fit for their work. Christmas and New Year's Day are universal holidays in this district, and generally the wakes or feasts of the different villages, and the races in their respective neighbourhoods, for example at Worsley, Eccles Wakes, at St Helens and Haydock, the Newton Races, the Manchester Races also, which occur during Whitsuntide, attract an immense number of colliers . . . .

Life in the mining villages changed gradually after the Mines Act of 1842 which forbade the employment of women down the mines (though not at the pit-brows) and of children under the age of ten. Mining continued to be a hard and dangerous life even when only adult males were exposed to the chief risks. In the 1850s over 300 were killed in Lancashire. The Ince Hall disaster of 1854 in which, among other failures, the ventilation system broke down, claimed 59. Pit safety and miners' insurance improved after another bad series of accidents in 1869-71. This was the human cost of the 10 million tons of Lancashire coal mined each year in the mid-nineteenth century, which reached a record of 26 million tons in 1908.

English society in the seventeenth and eighteenth centuries provided a safety net for social failures. This was 'the Poor Law'. Rather than being one particular law, the Poor Law comprised a whole series of Acts and local byelaws carried out at different times and in different places between 1601 and 1834. Its three major features were the laws of settlement, outdoor relief and the workhouse. The laws of settlement attempted to provide some check on mobility, but, failing in this, they ensured that at least one parish was responsible for everyone born in England and Wales. If in doubt, a person applying for relief could always be removed to his or her place of birth and that parish would be held responsible for relief. Outdoor relief ordinarily took the form of food or money doles to individuals or families in temporary distress. The old, the orphans, the sick, the disabled and the lunatic were looked after in the poorhouse or workhouse. In practice each parish was left to devise its own scheme of poor relief within guidelines laid down by Acts of Parliament as interpreted by the local magistrates.

The rising costs of poor relief during and after the French Wars of 1793-1815 led to a complete reappraisal of the Poor Law. The labourers were said to be demoralized by indiscriminate doles, and suggestions for the total removal of any such public safety net led to the Poor Law Amendment Act of 1834. This set up a central Poor Law Commission and reformed local administration by grouping parishes into unions. It also introduced the principle of the workhouse test by which relief was to be only available inside the workhouse, and was concerned to make conditions in these new union workhouses 'less eligible' (less desirable) than life outside. The legislators hoped thus to cut the cost of relief by reducing the number of applicants.

The Act of 1834 was primarily intended to help the arable areas of the south and east where pauperism had become a way of life. It was felt in Lancashire to have little relevance to local needs. There was a labour shortage in the county, the reverse of the problem of the counties where the Speenhamland system — the most common system of outdoor relief between 1795 and 1834 — had flourished. Most Lancastrians rejected the idea that a temporary depression in trade should force a man and his family into the workhouse or 'Bastille' as it was commonly nicknamed. Chadwick's scheme for large new union workhouses to replace the old parish workhouses, established under the Act of 1723, seemed wasteful and inhumane. Consequently, Lancashire unions were slow to co-operate with the Poor Law Commission and its successor the Poor Law Board. Many of the old parish workhouses continued in operation long after 1834, even though their condition in many cases justified the reforms which the Commissioners urged.

The condition of one of these old-style workhouses is illustrated by the scandals that broke around the heads of the Bolton Union Board of Guardians in the winter of 1842-3. Bolton Union had inherited several workhouses, but its largest was in Fletcher Street, Great Bolton. That particular workhouse consisted of 13 cottages, mainly grouped around a yard. At Christmas 1842, Fletcher Street workhouse was full to bursting. Three hundred paupers occupied its cottages, crammed 20 to 25 in a cottage. There were only 119 beds in all, so families slept together in one bed as they would have done at home, and the single beds were reserved for fever patients. Single men and women were kept in separate accommodation.

By day as well as by night the workhouse was run on the family system. Each cottage had its dayroom downstairs, and there were rooms for washing and cooking. The children under ten were sent off to infant school every morning and afternoon, and the older ones attended Sunday school. Most adults were employed in picking old ropes for oakum. Some of the women did the cooking and cleaning. Some of the men did odd jobs outside the house: one was a mangle turner, another a roadmender. Some had special jobs in the house as barber or nurse. There was considerable freedom to come and go as the inmates pleased, although official pressure caused some restrictions. From August 1842 no resident pauper was allowed back into the house after 7 pm. Similarly, no leave was granted for church attendance on Sundays, because experience had shown that the inmates only made straight for neighbouring alehouses and came back drunk and disorderly.

There was little doubt that the Fletcher Street premises were inadequate and overcrowded, but this was true of many Lancashire workhouses, especially after some had been closed on the recommendation of the Commissioners. A series of incidents in 1842 brought the principal Bolton workhouse to the public notice. In July the Guardians had had the embarrassment of the death of an old woman 'from want of food' while in receipt of a two shilling weekly allowance. She had refused the Board's advice to go into the workhouse, but the case provoked a Commissioners' inquiry. In the stir which followed one former occupant of the workhouse interrupted a meeting of the Guardians, opened up a handkerchief and threw two 'whacks' of bread onto the table in front of them, in protest at the bread ration at Fletcher Street.

The scandalous state of the workhouse was only fully revealed by the death of Ann Heywood. A 73-year-old inmate, she had been ill for almost a year and had become 'bedfast' in the workhouse hospital. There she was looked after by the nurse, the surgeon occasionally giving her a pill or some castor oil. One evening in December 1842, she had been rather quieter than usual, and the nurse, who was a good deal the worse for drink, put a pillow over her face and told another pauper that she was dead. With help, the nurse dragged her down to the dead-house and was laying her out when she began to stir. One of the paupers sent for the governor, and she was taken back to the sick room where she died later that evening. The Guardians were loath to sack the drunken nurse, Molly Davenport, because not only was she too a pauper, but she had a surprising immunity to the fever which had already carried off two nurses in quick succession. Above all she was not in a fit state to quit the workhouse.

The failure to dismiss Molly Davenport caused great unrest among the other occupants. Three paupers went on strike when a man, said to be insane, was brought to Fletcher Street and locked up. The strikers said that they wanted no more murders. James Flitcroft, a cartsheet marker, with a lunatic cousin in the workhouse, interrupted a meeting of the Guardians with accusations of maltreatment and a display of lice picked off his cousin. The interruption was not taken very seriously by one of the Guardians:

James Flitcroft: I will send this bundle of lice to the Commissioners. *Mr Shaw:* Do lad, they're Bourton greys; they'll be good layers. (from: *Bolton Chronicle,* 17 December 1842)

When, however, Dr Heap checked his charges, he found the infestation to be general. There seemed to be no easy solution, for the governor said he had no power to order haircuts.

The Tory leadership of the Guardians regarded the protests as a Radical plot. They welcomed a Commissioners' inquiry to help clear the air. The Commissioner, as might be expected, condemned the whole setup. He found that six children had scarlet fever, several had 'bad eyes', and one woman had consumption.

Change came slowly. A workhouse committee was established to keep a closer eye on Fletcher Street. Tighter discipline was to be exerted. The master and his wife were to preside at meals. Men and women were to be separated while picking oakum. The able-bodied were told to leave. The drunken nurse was dismissed and only replaced on a temporary basis. The workhouse yard was cleaned out, a special washhouse made and new privies installed.

Such improvements brought Fletcher Street more into line with the principles of the 1834 Act, but it still fell far short of what the Commissioners wanted. The latter urged the construction of a single workhouse for the whole union. Resistance to such a bastille was slow to die, but the new ideas were eventually victorious in the new Bolton Union workhouse, built at Fishpool at a cost of £33,000 between 1858 and 1861.

Unlike its principal predecessor at Fletcher Street, the new Bolton Union workhouse (now Bolton General Hospital) lived up in full to the ideals of the New Poor Law. 'The style of the architecture is

Italian, but the building is also plain, substantial and effective', wrote one journalist. Bolton had its bastille at last. Its inmates were classified and uniformed, disciplined and well-worked. The nature of that work had not changed: 'The "test" is applied in the shape of oakum picking, wood chopping and corn grinding'. Nevertheless, the inmates were now clean, healthy and adequately fed. The new workhouse was well staffed. The officials included a chaplain, schoolmaster and schoolmistress as well as a master and mistress for the general administration of the place. At the school cottages in the grounds, 'useful' and industrial occupations were taught, including tailoring, weaving and mat-making. The workhouse had its own chapel and cemetery as well. There was now no need, once inside the new workhouse, ever to leave it. This was the great deterrent, which frightened most people from ever darkening its doors, if they could possibly avoid it. Chadwick called it the principle of 'less eligibility'.

In 1861, the newly established poor law policy was blown completely off course by the outbreak of the American Civil War. The Northern blockade of Southern ports prevented the exportation of raw cotton, and the Lancashire cotton industry was by degrees brought to a complete standstill. In all cotton towns thousands were thrown onto poor relief. In Preston nearly all the 25,000 cotton workers became dependent on the paltry 1s 5d (7p) from the Guardians and 5d (2p) from the Relief Fund. Outdoor relief was back again with a vengeance. Edwin Waugh, the Lancashire journalist and poet, found such cases as the family of 13 whose joint wages from the mill had amounted to 80s (£4.00) a week and whose relief was only 6s (30p). More money could be earned at the stoneyard, where 1s (5p) was paid for breaking a ton of stones or wheeling three tons in a barrow. Others were set to work in laying out Avenham Park. Many cotton workers thought twice about ruining their hands with such heavy work, but they had little choice. Some, however, only had to undergo an education test, or attend the temporary schools which were set up. Many had to sell all their possessions, and there was a good deal of informing about those suspected of having savings bank accounts intact. Many were forced to move into the cheapest possible housing, in the courts of the town centres. Money poured in from all over the country to help finance food kitchens and sewing committees. Conditions began to improve in 1864. It was some time before the mill-hands had recovered their savings and their pride, but many had learnt to read and write. Their patience was seen as an example of working class reliability and, in return, Parliament gave all borough householders the vote in 1867.

Rapid population growth between 1780 and 1850 put enormous pressure on all social facilities, especially in the towns. Schools and churches, magistrates, vestries and town councils, all found it impossible to keep abreast of the problems brought by the Industrial Revolution. Literacy rates declined in towns, along with church attendance, public order and cleanliness. A start was made in the 1830s, with the first state grants to education, the reform of local government and the institution of local police forces.

The cholera epidemic of 1831-2 forced the towns to take action on public health. Local committees, called Boards of Health, encouraged the poor to wash themselves and to whitewash their homes; benevolent ladies made 'anti-cholera flannel waistcoats'; fast days and special church services were held, as in time of war. The cholera took its toll in certain towns and then subsided. Voluntary efforts could not be sustained; legal powers, administrative machinery and medical knowledge were all wanting. The core of activists in each town collected information and supplied the Health of Towns Commission with many grim statistics for its massive reports of 1844 and 1845. Chadwick's own Sanitary Report of 1842 and the efforts of certain individual towns, like Liverpool, also helped prepare the way for reform. The Public Health Act of 1848, which was finally provoked by the second cholera panic in that year, allowed ratepayers to set up elected Boards of Health with powers to levy rates and make improvements with the help of expert advice from the General Board of Health in London.

In 1846, Liverpool, where 53% of children under five years old died, acquired statutory powers for the corporation to cope with sewerage and water supply, and appointed Dr Duncan its first Medical Officer of Health. The town, however, was overtaken by events. The Irish Potato Famine of 1845-6 turned the ebb and flow of Irish migration to Liverpool into a flood. By the end of June 1847, 300,000 Irish had landed, many of whom were desperately ill with 'famine fever' (typhus), and local medical provision was overwhelmed. Measles, smallpox, scarlatina (scarlet fever) and influenza swept through the town in the wake of typhus. The town was only just beginning to recover, when in December 1848, one of the children of an Irish family came ashore from a steamer and was shortly afterwards certified as a cholera case. In 1849 over 5,000 people in Liverpool died of cholera. The epidemic returned to Lancashire again in 1854 and 1866.

Improvement in public health was slow. Thanks to the Act of 1848 and the special arrangements made by larger towns, four-fifths of Lancashire's population was covered by competent health authorities by 1858. Provision of essential sewers and clean water was, however, an extremely expensive business. Hundreds of thousands of pounds had to be raised on the rates. Frequent opposition from ratepayers forced local reforming politicians and borough engineers to act cautiously. Reservoirs came first: Ormskirk could boast the first completed scheme in Lancashire in 1854; Bolton and Liverpool had piped water supplies by 1857. Other towns followed in the 1860s. Scavenging, or street-cleaning, improved. More streets were paved, and bye-laws were passed laying down minimum requirements for new streets of houses. Sewerage schemes were gradually implemented: Preston was successfully sewered by 1862, and over £200,000 had been spent in Liverpool by 1858. Yet even with such efforts, death rates remained obstinately high. Liverpool's was still over 30 per thousand in the mid-1870s. Eradication of poverty was the answer; it was also the greatest obstacle.

What was life like in rural Lancashire in the first half of Victoria's reign? By 1831 only one in ten Lancashire families were described as 'chiefly employed in agriculture'. By 1861 only 6% of the population were included in the agricultural class. Lancashire had been industrialized before the railways. Even the number of people who were engaged in part-time farming — like hand-loom weavers — fell in these years.

Life had not changed a great deal for those who had stayed on the farms. Many of the workers still lived with their employers and were described as 'farm servants'. According to Jonathan Binns, the Lancaster surveyor, in 1851: 'the servants mostly sit down to a good supply of oatmeal porridge, bread and cheese, pork and bacon, and some farmers kill a sheep occasionally, and a cow for winter use: the farmer often joins the servants at the same table'. This was the traditional custom which had already disappeared in many parts of the country. Lancashire farmhouses were equally old-fashioned:

The house is often very inadequate, the windows in many of the small farm-houses having no opening at all for the admission of

150

fresh air, or having only a small pane opening to the extent of six or eight inches. The upper rooms want partitions for keeping members of the family properly select. The floors are often so broken, and many of them without boards or flags, as to render cleanliness impossible. The dairy is inconveniently small, often exposed to the sun, and has also to be used for pantry and other purposes. (J. Binns, *Notes on the Agriculture of Lancashire,* 1851)

Contemporary commentators did not feel that the old farmhouses, which survive in great numbers even today, were in keeping with a modern farmer's status. Nor were they particularly impressed by the living conditions of the married labourers. In much of rural Lancashire, particularly in the west, these lived in:

miserable mud cottages open to the thatch, without light, except through a little hole in the mud wall, which goes by the name of window, and once had small pieces of glass in it . . . . Some of these cottages are rude, picturesque objects, very like the Irish cabin — their chimneys of all shapes, being composed of sticks and clay stuck upon the thatch, the floor only clay or soil, and the door too low to admit a middle-sized man without stooping.

(*Notes on the Agriculture of Lancashire*)

Fuel was cheap for the Lancashire labourer, and his wages were higher than in the south, but, as Binns points out, he often had no garden in which to keep pigs or grow potatoes. Life gradually improved in the course of the nineteenth century, as allotments were introduced and 'model' cottages were built by exemplary landlords. This was some compensation for the loss of the wastes where the labourer had once been able to keep geese. Village missions were established by Nonconformist — often Methodist — preachers initially in a rented room and later in a chapel built with local funds. Village schools were normally set up by a benevolent squire or parson. Both missions and schools helped to improve the quality of life in rural areas.

Farming methods in the mid-nineteenth century were mainly dictated by long tradition. Long-horns had been replaced by short-horns on the northern cattle-breeding farms, but wooden-frame ploughs still predominated where there was arable cultivation. Plough teams were tethered in line rather than abreast. Many Lancashire arable farmers took little notice of Arther Young, the agricultural journalist of the late eighteenth century who had proclaimed the advantages of the Norfolk system of four-course rotation, and concentrated on producing oats and potatoes. Their great asset was the ready availability of town 'night-soil', which was used in large quantities in the Ormskirk area, thanks to the Leeds–Liverpool Canal. As Lord Derby, later Prime Minister, told the county agricultural society, 'where there's muck there's money'.

In 1850 there were one or two large modern farms of several hundred acres which drew great praise from the pundits. Such farms exhibited all the features of the 'new husbandry'. They followed the four-course rotation, grew turnips like the best Norfolk farmers, eradicated hedgerows and redisposed ditches. Moreover they made use of the new technology, sowing with seed drills, threshing with steam engines and introducing tile drainage and pumping gear as the final solution of the problem of the peatmosses. The model farmers, backed by enthusiastic landlords, such as Lords Derby, Sefton and Burlington, spread guano and bonemeal on the land, erected new farm buildings, 'with commodious dwelling-houses, adapted to the status of the new occupiers'. In such new farmhouses there was no provision for the old farm servants. The labourers had to live out, but they benefited from the variety of extra work available. Later on, landowners built brick cottages for the labourers on the estate.

Such farms never became typical of the north-west in the nineteenth century. In the neighbourhood of big towns the emphasis was on milk production by small farms. In north Lancashire there was an emphasis on cattle-breeding. Such farms changed in the second half of the century when cattle-feed cake and a variety of new fertilisers were introduced. The system of farm servants, however, survived, especially on the medium-sized farms. The county's bias towards grass was strengthened by the agricultural depression in the last quarter of the century, when dairy produce for the towns became far more profitable than arable cultivation. This pattern was only changed in some parts of the county in the twentieth century, when two World Wars led to renewed demand for home-grown corn.

9 LATE VICTORIAN AND EDWARDIAN HEY-DAY

The England of the past has been an England of reserved, silent men, dispersed in small towns, villages, and country homes. The England of the future is an England packed tightly in such gigantic aggregations of population as the world has never before seen.

So C.F.G. Masterman described London in *The Condition of England* in 1902, but the problems of urbanization were equally pressing in Lancashire, whose population had topped four million in 1901, with a density of 2,000 per square mile.

Most of these four million people lived south of the Ribble. Even in south Lancashire the problem was not that of a single huge conurbation, but that of a plurality of towns of all sizes. Over a third of Lancastrians now lived in three cities — Liverpool, Manchester or Salford. By 1911 there were 17 county boroughs with populations of over 50,000 and 18 municipal boroughs with populations over 10,000, as well as a number of urban districts. Only one in 24 of the population lived in areas designated 'rural'. New towns continued to spring up, especially along the coast. Heysham and St Annes were the Edwardian mushroom towns, while between 1871 and 1911 Blackpool grew sixfold.

In spite of continued growth, Lancashire towns retained their individuality. Dialect and accent differed — as they still do — from one place to another, with mysterious linguistic frontiers like the one which separated Liverpool from other parts of south Lancashire. Immigration from Scotland, Wales, Ireland and other parts of England — not to mention the arrival of Russian, Italian and German immigrants — gave each town a distinct ethnic composition. Religious and racial divisions led to much communal stress, but in the long term they found comparatively peaceful expression in sporting rivalry especially on the football field.

Individuality frequently derived from history, but rarely from the distant past. Liverpool and Manchester took pride in their mediaeval origins, but Barrow was proud to be the creation of Victorian business acumen and imagination. Lancashire towns, with exceptions in the north, such as Garstang and Hawkshead, had a predominantly Victorian look, however ancient their charters. They were wealthier than they had ever been and they expressed their individuality in the different architectural styles of their public buildings. Liverpool showed a preference for classical styles, Manchester for Gothic. Rochdale's Town Hall was Gothic, Bolton's was classical. Lancashire towns had political characters too. On the Tory side were ranged Liverpool, Preston, Blackburn and the seaside towns. Among the Liberal towns were Oldham, Rochdale and Lancaster.

Lastly, and most importantly, was the character derived from local industry. 'Manchester man, Liverpool gentleman' was a quip which had once distinguished between the 'putter-out' and the import merchant, but came to imply much more. The inner ring of towns round Manchester, comprising Ashton, Oldham, Rochdale, Bury and a number of smaller centres, were all predominantly concerned with cotton-spinning. The outer ring of Burnley, Accrington, Blackburn and Preston constituted the weaving belt. The chief centres for bleaching, dyeing, printing and finishing were Bolton and Manchester. Manchester had lived down the quip, and had acquired direct access to its foreign markets by the building of the Manchester Ship Canal (completed in 1896). Smaller places had their own distinctive economic character. In the south, Wigan and Leigh, although both engaged in cotton, were more important as the centres of coal production. Warrington was renowned for leather, beer and soap, while the new towns of St Helens and Widnes were making fortunes for manufacturers of glass and chemicals. Further north, Horwich had become identified with railway workshops and Darwen for its bricks and tiles. North of the Ribble, Lancaster had become a trade name for oilcloth and linoleum, while Barrow, already famous for its haematite iron and steel works, was hitting Edwardian newspaper headlines with the regular launchings of 'dreadnoughts' from the Vickers shipyards.

Transport developments gave all the towns a ring of new suburbs.

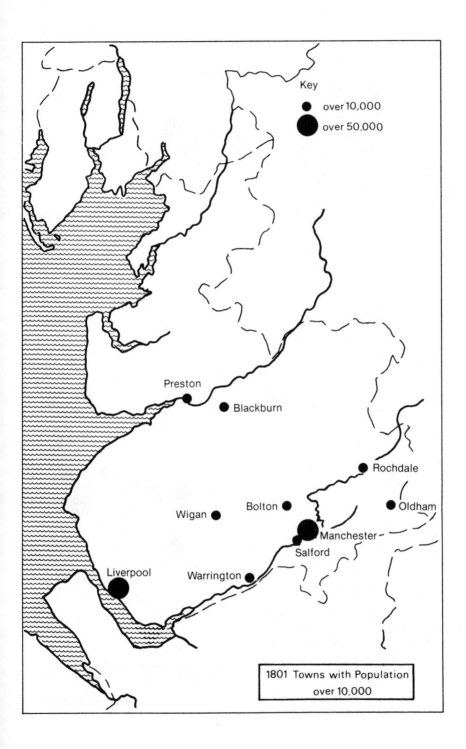

Key
● over 10,000
● over 50,000

Preston
Blackburn

Rochdale

Bolton
Wigan
Oldham

Manchester
Salford

Liverpool
Warrington

1801 Towns with Population
over 10,000

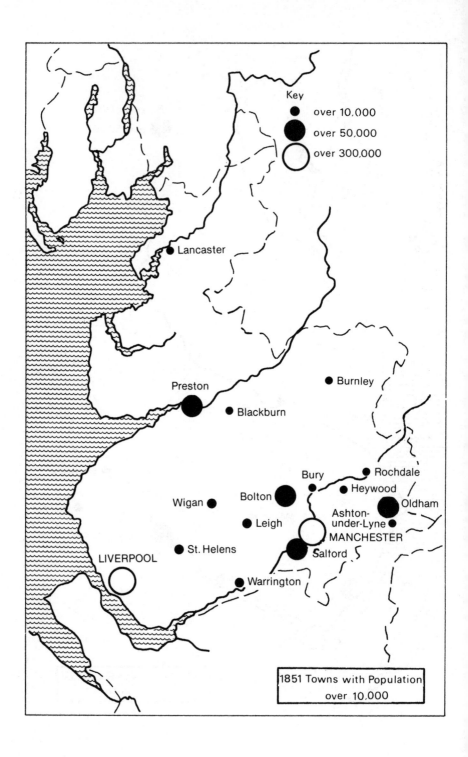

Key

● over 10,000

⬤ over 50,000

◯ over 300,000

Lancaster

Preston

Blackburn

Burnley

Bury

Rochdale

Heywood

Wigan

Bolton

Oldham

Leigh

Ashton-
under-Lyne

MANCHESTER

St. Helens

Saltord

LIVERPOOL

Warrington

1851 Towns with Population
over 10,000

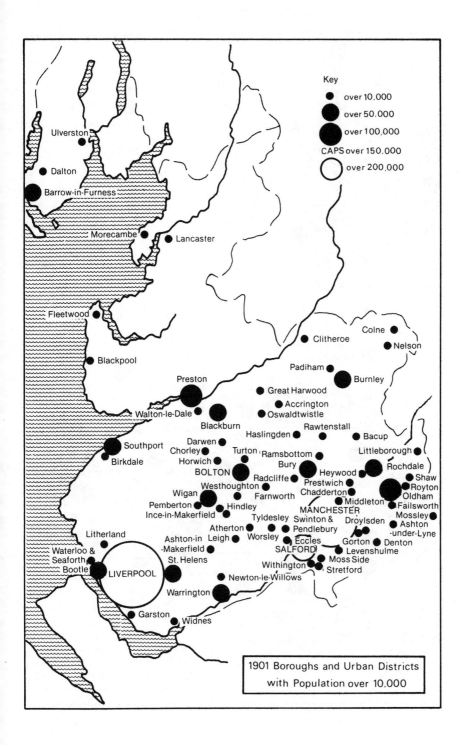

Key

● over 10,000

● over 50,000

● over 100,000

CAPS over 150,000

○ over 200,000

Ulverston

Dalton

Barrow-in-Furness

Morecambe

Lancaster

Fleetwood

Blackpool

Preston

Walton-le-Dale

Colne

Nelson

Padiham

Burnley

Clitheroe

Great Harwood

Accrington

Oswaldtwistle

Blackburn

Haslingden

Rawtenstall

Bacup

Southport

Darwen

Chorley

Horwich

Turton

Ramsbottom

Littleborough

Rochdale

Birkdale

BOLTON

Radcliffe

Bury

Heywood

Prestwich

Shaw

Royton

Oldham

Westhoughton

Farnworth

Chadderton

Middleton

Failsworth

Wigan

Hindley

MANCHESTER

Mossley

Pemberton

Ince-in-Makerfield

Tyldesley

Swinton &
Pendlebury

Droylsden

Ashton
-under-Lyne

Litherland

Atherton

Worsley

Eccles

Gorton

Denton

Waterloo &
Seaforth
Bootle

Ashton-in
-Makerfield

Leigh

SALFORD

Levenshulme

LIVERPOOL

St. Helens

Withington

Moss Side

Stretford

Newton-le-Willows

Warrington

Garston

Widnes

1901 Boroughs and Urban Districts
with Population over 10,000

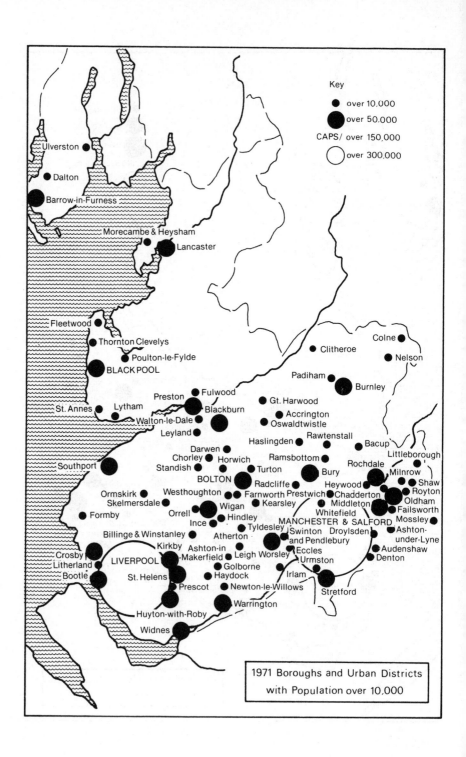

Key

● over 10,000

⬤ over 50,000

CAPS/ over 150,000

◯ over 300,000

Ulverston ●

● Dalton

⬤ Barrow-in-Furness

Morecambe & Heysham

⬤ Lancaster

Fleetwood ●

● Thornton Clevelys

● Poulton-le-Fylde

⬤ BLACKPOOL

St. Annes ●   ● Lytham

Colne ●

● Clitheroe   Nelson

Padiham ●   ⬤ Burnley

Preston   ● Fulwood

● Blackburn

Walton-le-Dale ●   ● Gt. Harwood

Leyland ●   ● Accrington

      ● Oswaldtwistle

Haslingden ●   ● Rawtenstall   ● Bacup

Darwen ●   Littleborough

Chorley ●   ● Horwich   Ramsbottom ●   Rochdale ●

Southport ⬤   Standish ●   ● Turton   ⬤ Bury   ● Milnrow

BOLTON   ● Radcliffe   Heywood ●   ● Shaw

Ormskirk ●   Westhoughton ●   ● Farnworth Prestwich ● Chadderton ● Royton

Skelmersdale ●   Middleton ●   Oldham

            ● Wigan   ● Kearsley   Whitefield ●   Failsworth

Formby ●   Orrell ●   ● Hindley   Mossley ●

      Ince ●   MANCHESTER & SALFORD

Billinge & Winstanley ●   Atherton ●   ● Tyldesley   Ashton-

      Kirkby ●   Swinton Droylsden ●   under-Lyne

Crosby ●   Ashton-in   Droylsden   Audenshaw ●

Litherland ●   LIVERPOOL -Makerfield ● Leigh Worsley ● Eccles ● Denton ●

Bootle ●   St. Helens   ● Golborne   Urmston

      ● Prescot   ● Haydock   Irlam ●

      Huyton-with-Roby   ● Newton-le-Willows   Stretford ⬤

      Widnes   ● Warrington

1971 Boroughs and Urban Districts
with Population over 10,000

158

Migration to the countryside was first made possible by suburban rail services. Some lines became electrified. The Mersey Railway was converted in 1903, and the important Liverpool–Southport link was electrified in the following year. Tramway services were developed — horse-drawn from the 1870s (Liverpool's dated from 1868) and electric from 1900-05 (although Blackpool had been operating an electric service from 1885, and Burnley had steam trams from 1881). A vast network of lines made it possible to travel by tram all over south Lancashire. The journey from Liverpool to Colne could be made in 18 hours. Trams were better for shorter distances and they were cheap enough to be a boon to all classes of the community. Ribbon development along main roads was no longer limited to big, detached villas. Builders now built terrace-housing for clerks and office workers on the outskirts of the big towns and even gave birth to new working-class suburbs such as Halliwell near Bolton.

In spite of these developments the bulk of the population still lived either in the town centres, in overcrowded courts and narrow dirty side streets or, a little further out, in long rows of uniform, red-brick cottages, separated by the wider, windier streets, laid out by builders in compliance with the bye-laws of the 1850s and 1860s. Town centres changed, with increasing shop and office development and street-widening. Local authorities sometimes took a lead in demolition, but were reluctant to supply housing for those made homeless by 'improvements'. Liverpool led the way in municipal housing developments in 1869, with its four-storey flats euphemistically christened 'St Martin's Cottages'. Manchester's scheme in Ancoats did not follow until 1889, and most town councils went no further than consultation and discussion. Without government aid, such schemes seemed economically prohibitive.

There were a number of 'slum' areas, especially in the big cities, where islands of poverty were formed by barriers such as railway embankments and canals. Yet, on the whole, the towns were remarkably well integrated communities, consisting mainly of mill-workers, craftsmen, corner shopkeepers, labourers and casual workers. To describe the industrialized urban environment simply as a 'slum' world is to recognize its dreary poverty and dirt, but to ignore its enormous variety and vitality.

Seebohm Rowntree calculated that about one third of the population of Edwardian York lived in poverty, and the situation in Lancashire towns was probably similar. Skilled men took home about

35s or 40s a week, but labourers received only half this amount. In the cotton industry women were paid about two thirds the men's rates. Real wages rose steadily from 1870 to 1900, declined somewhat between 1900 and 1910 and then rose once more as wages were increased in the boom of 1911-13.

Poverty was most frequent among the casual workers, dock labourers and street hawkers who congregated in the big cities, had no steady source of income, and lived on the edge of a world of crime, prison and the workhouse. Jerome Caminada, a Manchester police officer writing in the 1890s, described the inhabitants of the Manchester street world as 'curious, crawling, creeping figures . . . slinking away in their rags', condemned to the rough life of sweat shop and gin palace. Police supervision was much more thorough and extensive by the late nineteenth century, but when the police went on strike in Liverpool in 1919, all hell was let loose and the troops had to be called in.

Families with more than one member on a steady wage could usually expect to live respectably, if they were careful. The fact that by pooling their wages families could usually keep their members from the disgrace of the workhouse or crime, put a premium on family discipline. Father had a paramount position as the principal breadwinner, and he was treated with appropriate respect within the home, occupying the best chair and receiving priority at mealtimes. Mother was the lynch-pin of the family and the main source of comfort and advice to the children. If she went out to work she entrusted her youngest children to a childminder, perhaps an older relative or an elder daughter.

The daily routine for the millworker's family had not greatly changed since the middle of the nineteenth century. It began with the rattle on the bedroom window made by the long pole of the knocker-up at about 5 am. With only a drink of tea inside him and his breakfast in a square tin, the factory hand set off to arrive at his work by 6 am. After two hours there was a breakfast break of half an hour's duration, followed by another for dinner at 12.30 pm. If his wife worked too, a pie was fetched from a confectioner's or sent from home by one of the children. The hot potato pie (hot-pot) and pickled cabbage were washed down either with tea brewed at the mill canteen or with a jug of ale fetched, again by one of the children, from the local public house. At home after 5 pm tea — perhaps tripe and onions — soon followed. Then there was shopping to be done at the corner shop or at the increasingly popular 'Co-op' (originating in Toad Lane, Rochdale in 1844), where housewives could be sure of unadulterated goods, reliable services, and a chance of a dividend. Later, father met his friends at the 'local', although mother still had plenty of chores to do. The rapid growth of fried-fish shops in the late nineteenth century meant the occasional treat of a bought supper before going to bed. This was the routine brought by industrialism, and some of its features are still familiar today.

The side streets were full of the noise of children who played there for want of anywhere better. Back yards were too small, while parks were often distant and were sometimes for ornamental purposes only. As late as 1900 there were still many schools without playgrounds. All sorts of games were played, including singing-games such as 'There came three dukes a-riding'. There were fewer pets in 1900 than today, although canaries were popular and some children kept rabbits or white mice. Most families had a cat, and men kept ferrets for rabbiting and ratting, or whippets and pigeons for racing. Outbreaks of rabies, as in 1889, obliged the government to issue periodic orders for all dogs to be muzzled.

School attendance had been compulsory since 1876 and local officials did their best to enforce it. The school-leaving age was 10 from 1876 to 1899, and 12 from then until 1918 when it was raised to 14. State elementary schools, or 'Board Schools', were free to any child up to his fourteenth birthday. Many children were sent to school without footwear, and private funds were set up to provide them with clogs. Free school meals were provided by the local education committees after 1906, although voluntary funds had already started dinner schemes in some places. In hard times children might receive free breakfasts at school as well.

Elementary schools were characterized by huge classes (often of 60), deplorable sanitary arrangements and constant disruption. Town schools did not suffer the disruptions caused by haymaking, harvesting and potato planting and getting, but they were frequently decimated by epidemics of scarlet fever, measles, whooping cough and diphtheria. The health of village schools was not much better: that at Caton was closed no less than eight times because of epidemics between 1893 and 1907.

This was not an educational environment conducive to success. As Robert Roberts, a former pupil in Salford, wrote: 'With a deep consciousness of global possession, a grasp of the decalogue and modicum of knowledge we left in droves at the very first hour the law would allow and sought any job at all in factory, mill and shop' (R. Roberts, *The Classic Slum*, 1971). A very few, like Ernest Barker, obtained free places in the old grammar schools which had been revivified for the sons of shopkeepers and professional men in the course of the nineteenth century, with the curriculum still heavily biased towards the classics. In this way Barker, the son of a quarryman and a mill-girl, became, via Manchester Grammar School and Balliol, one of the great classical scholars of the twentieth century. Meanwhile girls' secondary education was even more neglected, and technical schools only began to make an impact after the Technical Instruction Act of 1889.

Middle-class pressure had led to the provision of colleges, like Owens at Manchester (1851) and Queen's at Liverpool (1857) to teach traditional university subjects. In 1880 Owens College became the nucleus of the federal Victoria University, and in 1903 the colleges at Manchester and Liverpool both acquired independent university status, with large financial assistance from local merchants and manufacturers. The first women students were admitted at Manchester in 1883, but it was not till 1899 that every department of the college became open to them. Although no longer male preserves, such institutions were of necessity very middle-class, and it was not until 1903, with the founding of the Workers' Education Association, that university teaching was at last brought to working people.

Meanwhile free libraries were set up with the help of benefactors like E.R. Harris, a solicitor, at Preston and the American steel baron, Andrew Carnegie, at Blackpool, Nelson and elsewhere. By 1901 an estimated 3,000 people were using the Harris reading-room at Preston. Membership was restricted to those over 14 until 1906, but many children, like Ernest Barker, had access to Sunday school libraries and such cheap popular series as the Cassells 3d National Library.

Death rates fell dramatically in the closing decades of the nineteenth century, although the dangers to life during infancy resisted all efforts of the medical officers of health (appointed to every Board of Health after 1875). It was still not unknown for babies to be suffocated in their mothers' beds. In a 'two-up and two-downer', families still shared beds, and a number of the poorest families lived in one room. Navvies away on a job had to share with workmates or strangers. As one navvy mildly complained of a Lancaster lodging-house, 'with four in a bed (and two of them drunk) it isn't very comfortable'

Recruiting offices during the Boer War revealed startling facts about Lancashire schoolchildren, such as 'hair and body lice, decaying teeth, suppurating ears and deafness, ringworm and tuberculosis'. Fevers carried off many, in spite of heroic attempts by housewives, who wore themselves out in the battle against grime and bugs, aided by corporation whitewash and lime and advice from Ladies' Health Societies. There was, however, little that could be done to offset the effects of smoke pollution, heavy fogs and long hours in the damp hot atmosphere of a cotton mill or, indeed, the effect of over-work in any job.

Malnutrition remained a major problem, although more often from ignorance of the essentials of a nutritious diet than from bare want. Bread and potatoes still formed the major ingredients of most meals. Food had to be tasty. Children were kept going between inadequate meals with treacle butties, and adults liked large quantities of sauce and pickles with their food. Boiled ham was highly regarded, but was reserved for weekends, special occasions and, of course, funerals. Cooked meat was still a rarity, although roast Argentinian beef was beginning to appear on Sunday dinner tables. Fresh fish — particularly Icelandic cod — was also becoming popular, and most street-corners had a chip shop by 1900. Little fruit was consumed: bananas and tomatoes were thought to be positively harmful. Milk was obtainable quite cheaply from roundsmen with their huge cans or 'kitters', but was often dirty or adulterated. The first dispensary to make clean milk available for nursing mothers was opened in St Helens in 1899. Tap water was still not entirely trusted, and tea was undoubtedly the favourite drink. Housewives kept the tea-kettle boiling at all hours, and tea-poisoning was a genuine hazard.

By the end of the nineteenth century the range of patent and quack remedies available for various ailments was wider than ever. Medical advertisers had access to an enormous market through the popular press and provided an important part of newspaper revenue. The classic success story was that of 'Doctor' Thomas Beecham of St Helens who, thanks to the successful national advertising of his pills, was producing nine million pills a day by 1890.

Meanwhile late Victorian Lancashire saw the proliferation of

163

hospitals with operating theatres, special children's wings and dental sections. Isolation hospitals for the treatment of victims of infectious diseases were also established. In addition, from the late 1880s, district nursing associations were set up to take hospital hygiene and care into private homes. Following Liverpool's example of 1897, many towns began to employ professional female health visitors. By such means some of the worst killers, such as cholera and smallpox were eliminated, and the standards of child care slowly improved. At the same time, MOHs campaigned for more sanitary housing and more water closets.

The struggle against drink provoked far more contemporary interest and controversy than that against disease. Heavy drinking was a major social problem, and restrictions on licensing hours were light. Apart from the Act of 1872 which closed public houses for six hours a day at the discretion of the magistrates, no further progress was made in the imposition of closer control before the First World War, except in the case of juvenile drinking. In 1908 it became illegal for children under 14 to enter a bar, and therefore 'taking out' was restricted to special 'jug and bottle' departments.

Clearance of town-centre slums considerably reduced the number of licensed premises. The new suburban pubs were more spacious and, with their billiard tables and bowling greens, aimed at destroying the temperance image of public houses as dens of vice. Yet the bald facts of the situation may be illustrated from Preston, the birthplace of teetotalism. Although 14 inns had been demolished there in the 1890s, in 1901 there were still 13 breweries and one licensed house to every 250 inhabitants.

The physical presence of church and chapel was as imposing as that of the public house in Lancashire towns. Many of the buildings had been put up or enlarged between 1850 and 1914, as part of an enormous effort to catch up with the growth of the population. In spite of this, a large proportion of the people, especially in the cities, did not attend any place of worship. Nevertheless, the various aspects of church life, from Sunday Schools to Pleasant Sunday Afternoons — where working men could enjoy a reading or recital and a cup of tea — flourished as never before. In smaller places such activities dominated the life of the community. In the large towns a strong sense of competition was engendered between Anglicans, Nonconformists (by 1900 known as Free Churchmen) and Roman Catholics. Denominations showed their political muscle at election times, but interest also focused on the turn-out for processions of witness — through the streets with banners and bands — held on May Day or at Whitsuntide. Roman Catholic processions were swelled by the Irish after the Potato Famine and by Italian immigrants at the turn of the century. Violence continued to be a feature of sectarian feelings, sometimes sparked off by travelling lecturers, but increasingly institutionalized in the kind of rivalry that has existed between the football clubs of Liverpool and Everton. There was a strong Mormon presence in Liverpool in the 1840s, but many emigrated to the United States. The growing Jewish population in Manchester added a new dimension to the religious scene.

Families imposed strong moral constraints on their members. High moral standards were a defence against economic disaster and a guarantee of social respectability. On the one hand they produced a strong sense of honesty and neighbourliness, on the other they gave rise to an over-developed censoriousness towards sex. Funerals were among the most important of family occasions. The family went into mourning and brought out the deceased's savings from the burial club or friendly society to pay for the expenses. A pauper's burial was a great disgrace but, for the provident, funerals meant new clothes for the children, a ham tea for all, and something stronger afterwards for the adults. The funerals of the great were witnessed with awe. Queen Victoria's was marked by the shutting of shops and hundreds of memorial services. For Lancastrians she had held a special place, toasted as 'the Queen, Duke of Lancaster', even though she disliked this odd amalgamation of titles.

Many Lancashire working-class householders received the vote in 1867; householders in rural and suburban areas were enfranchised in 1884. Great excitement was aroused by general elections, partly because the results were often close, and partly because candidates were more genuinely local than today. Political clubs abounded, and public meetings were well attended. Conservative or Unionist strength in Lancashire in the last quarter of the nineteenth century was due to the reforming tradition of families like the Crosses and Asshetons — who had an important influence on the social reforms of Disraeli's government of 1874-80 — combined with strong racial and religious hostility towards the Roman Catholic Irish. Brewers and publicans backed Tory candidates, while the temperance men and Nonconformists came out for the Liberals. In 1906 the latter triumphed because of their identification with Free Trade, which was regarded as vital to the health of the cotton industry. Labour made its first major impact in the 1906 election. Keir Hardie and Philip Snowden breached the Tory strongholds of Preston and Blackburn, and the earl of Derby's heir was defeated at Westhoughton. Labour benefited from its close association with the trade unions, particularly the weavers and miners. The cotton industry as a whole was highly unionized, and, after the employers, led by Charles Macara, and the spinners, led by James Maudsley, had accepted a three-tier system of arbitration in the Brooklands Agreement of 1893, there were only two major stoppages before the First World War.

Women as well as unions were now taking a more active part in politics. It was in Manchester in 1903 that Emmeline Pankhurst, the widow of a radical barrister, and her two daughters, Christabel and Sylvia, together founded the Women's Social and Political Union. Open-air meetings were held during wakes weeks in the towns around Manchester, and it was after interrupting Sir Edward Grey and Winston Churchill in the Manchester Free Trade Hall in 1906 that Christabel served her first prison sentence. Soon after this the focus of suffragette activities shifted to London.

Late Victorian prosperity brought the seaside within reach of most Lancashire families. Wakes or holiday weeks had become established practice in the mill towns, and part of the week was usually spent by the sea. Blackpool was the most popular of the resorts, with up to 20,000 visitors on any day in the season. Excursion trains brought people in groups from mill or chapel for day trips, although increasing numbers of the better-off could afford to stay the night. Cut-throat competition among boarding-house keepers meant that a bed could be obtained for as little as a shilling a night.

Blackpool boomed in the 1890s. A 'tripper' who saw the third pier opened in 1893, would have seen the completed Blackpool Tower (all 518 ft (158m) of it) the next year. In 1895 the Empire Theatre was opened, followed a year later by the Big Wheel and Empress Ballroom, and the Alhambra in 1899. Also that year, the North Shore promenade was completed and that on the South Shore was widened and rebuilt in 1905. Apart from all the traditional forms of seaside entertainment — Punch and Judy shows, fortune tellers and donkey rides — Blackpool specialized in providing the best artists and the latest inventions of the day. Sousa, Caruso and Houdini all performed in Edwardian Blackpool; and there were special trials for both motor cars and aeroplanes. The resort's first cinema, the Colosseum, was opened in 1905, although music hall variety was still the most popular evening entertainment. So far did this transcend class barriers that when King George V and Queen Mary visited the Earl of Derby at Knowsley in July 1913, they were entertained by 20 vaudeville artistes, including George Formby senior who sang 'quaint Lancashire dialect songs'.

Enthusiasm for football seemed equally classless. Lancashire teams emerged from a mixed background of old boys', Sunday school and works teams. When the professional Football League was founded in 1888, six of the twelve founding members were local clubs: Accrington Stanley, Blackburn Rovers, Bolton Wanderers, Burnley, Everton and Preston North End. With admission charges as low as 3d or 4d (2p) in the late 1880s, and with Saturday afternoons free, thousands turned out to watch. Star status was already being accorded to individual players, but wages were limited by the ceiling of £4 a week basic pay, imposed by the Football Association in 1900.

Cricket, too, developed as a spectator sport in the last years of the nineteenth century. The first day of the Roses match (first held in 1867) in August 1895 was watched by 25,000 people. By 1914 Lancashire had been county champions five times, and the county captain, Archie Maclaren, still held the record for the highest score in first-class cricket — his 424 runs at Taunton in 1895. Horse-racing also caught the popular imagination, and thousands followed the turf successes of Edward VII and Lord Derby in the sports pages of the new halfpenny press. Meanwhile cycling clubs were opening urban eyes to that world of rural north Lancashire so vividly portrayed in the writings of Beatrix Potter.

The leaders of county society were still the earls of Derby, Sefton and Crawford and Balcarres. The Derby inheritance of 70,000 acres brought in a gross rental of £300,000 a year. Death duties had not yet made major inroads into such fortunes, although Lloyd George's budget of 1909 was an omen of things to come. In 1910 the staff at Knowsley included 38 domestic servants and 39 gardeners, and, with royal visits and huge shooting parties, household expenditure amounted to nearly £50,000 a year. Bearing in mind the spread of the Derby estates, it was hardly surprising that the earl was referred to as 'King of Lancashire'.

10 THE TWENTIETH CENTURY

Before the First World War Lancashire had gloried in the strength of two of the country's major industries, cotton and coal. The war stretched coal to its full capacity, while cotton suffered from a shortage of man-power and a reduction in shipping space. The ensuing peace exposed the industry's underlying problems. Loss of export markets in textiles continued, as India, Britain's largest pre-war market, became virtually self-sufficient, and competitors such as Japan and Italy proved more efficient with newer machines, lower wages and better industrial organization. Coal deposits were running out, and the industry was beset by over-manning and low productivity. Many concerns were too small, in spite of reorganization, to survive.

Streamlining and readjustment to postwar conditions were painfully slow. In human terms these meant wage-cuts and unemployment. The miners' wages were cut in 1919, 1921 and 1926. The proposal for wage-cuts in 1929 sparked off the General Strike, but it only lasted nine days and demonstrated the weakness of the TUC. The miners' strike lasted another six months, but, in the end, the miners' leaders were forced to accept wage reductions. Union membership declined, and loss of funds made further action in the near future impossible.

In 1929 came the Wall Street Crash and the world slump. Unemployment in Britain jumped from 10% in 1929 to 21% in 1931. It struck hardest in the mining areas. At Wigan, unemployment rose to 35% in 1931, and at Hindley as many as 42% were out of work even in 1934, for many uneconomic pits were closed altogether.

The hopelessness of the unemployed miner and his family found a chronicler and a champion in the writer, George Orwell (Eric Blair), whose *The Road to Wigan Pier*, published in 1937, was an eye-opener to many who had never seen the areas devastated by lack of work. Orwell estimated that the average income of a family out of work was 30s (£1.50) a week, of which about a quarter went on rent. Along with the dole went the means test or 'meanest test' as it was nicknamed, by which the whole family's income was investigated to assess the amount of relief due to the unemployed. 'Luxury' items such as pianos had to be sold; tale-telling about unsold possessions and additional sources of income gave rise to much ill-will and occasional violence. One man struck the Pemberton relieving officer with a shovel when his relief was reduced from 27s (£1.35) to 23s (£1.15), after it was discovered that he had a paying lodger. The term 'lodger' even extended to elderly parents in receipt of pensions, who, in some cases, had to seek lodgings to prevent their children's dole from being cut.

As Orwell noted, the miner's weekly dole was not spent to best advantage. Nearly half the 32s (£1.60) of one miner's family of four had to go on rent, clothing club, fuel and power. Of the remaining half spent on food:

> The miner's family spend only tenpence a week on green vegetables and tenpence halfpenny on milk (remember that one of them is a child less than three years old), and nothing on fruit; but they spend one and nine on sugar (about eight pounds of sugar, that is) and a shilling on tea. . . . The basis of their diet, therefore, is white bread and margarine, corned beef, sugared tea, and potatoes — an appalling diet.

Orwell discovered nothing new, but he reached a wider public than many in pointing out the dangerous consequences for health of the combination of poverty and dietetic ignorance.

Unemployment was a long-drawn-out affair in the mining areas. With this in mind it is perhaps surprising how few moved away from Wigan to look for new jobs. From 1921 to 1931 Wigan's population fell by only 4,000 to just over 85,000. The fact that many women worked at cotton mills which went on short time, but did not entirely close down, is one explanation. These jobs helped to provide an anchor for whole families. After drastic wage-cuts, many miners were not much worse off economically out of work than in.

Efforts to provide alternative work in the neighbourhood were not very successful. Wigan corporation produced a scheme for clearing slag-heaps with unemployed labour, but the Ministry of Labour was not empowered to give financial support. Very little new industry came into the town in the period. A few men profited from the 'Upholland Experiment', by which retraining for semi-skilled jobs was provided at Wigan Technical Institute but its work was looked on with suspicion by the rest of the community. The unemployed were somewhat envious, while those still in work or self-employed feared competition. The Experiment did not get under way until the late 1930s and, although successful with its membership, only solved the problems of a small proportion of Wigan's unemployed.

Demoralization was perhaps the worst result of unemployment. The unemployed went picking coal and hung about at street corners. The public library reading-room became a popular place to go. Orwell shared a lodging-house with a man who did nothing all day except read the newspapers. The advertisers aimed their wares at such unfortunates. 'Half your difficulties are illusions', encouraged one advertisement for patent pills. 'Ill health makes them seem real.' There were not many clubs for the unemployed, but evening classes were popular, and billiard halls and cinemas were packed out. Orwell commented on the cheapness of Wigan cinema seats: 'You can always get a seat for fourpence, and at the matinee at some houses you can even get a seat for twopence'. In the summer of 1931, when 10,000 men and 4,000 women in Wigan were unemployed, a little dole money was well spent watching Wee Georgie Wood in *The Black Hand Gang* or Jean Harlow in *Hell's Angels*. The town had a number of cinemas, and some changed their programme on Thursday to show at least two main features a week. Amateur sports clubs flourished, and attendance at rugby league and cricket matches rose too.

Other issues and causes concerned the public as much as unemployment in the summer and autumn of 1931. Archbishop Downey of Liverpool addressed a rally in Springfield Park to raise money for the new Roman Catholic cathedral, which at a cost of £3 million was intended to be larger in area than Trafalgar Square and taller than Big Ben. No more than the crypt was ever completed. A few weeks later, Archbishop Temple visited Wigan Parish Church and preached on the themes of self-denial and steadfastness in the faith. The churches were deeply concerned about disarmament, and two big rallies were held in Wigan to canvass support in advance of the Disarmament Conference which was to be held in Geneva the following year.

Politicians were in general dumbfounded by the economic problems of the day. The resignation of the Labour Government, on the issue of the reduction of the dole, brought in the National Government, led by Ramsay Macdonald and Stanley Baldwin, and most Labour MPs went into opposition. The general election of 1931 confirmed this new government with a huge majority, but Wigan again voted Labour. There was a small following for the Communists, whose sporadic street activities contrasted markedly with the general apathy and quiet. The local press took it all very much in its stride. The weekly diet of motor-traffic accidents and violations of the 30mph speed limit for buses and lorries makes 1931 reporting seem surprisingly up-to-date. The fall in drunkenness, the increase in divorce and the rise of dance halls and cinemas, all showed how much life had changed since the Great War.

Meanwhile big rehousing schemes were started by most Lancashire towns to try to solve the problem of slums. For those who could find jobs (and there was little unemployment in such areas as Leyland or the Fylde), the 1930s brought a big improvement in the standard of living.

The Second World War put an immediate end to unemployment and provided a sense of national purpose which was eagerly grasped by those who had felt life to be aimless in the depression. Churchill's speeches were echoed by less eloquent but equally sincere voices. One newspaper editor wrote in December 1940: 'The war has brought with it a stirring of the social conscience, and there is greater fellowship today than there ever has been in the history of our island race'. Such words were very soon to be put to the test, especially in Liverpool and Manchester, for, in the nights leading up to Christmas 1940, the German Luftwaffe brought Hitler's *blitzkrieg* to the two principal cities of the north-west. Liverpool was pounded on the nights of 20-23 December and again, even more heavily, in the first week of May 1941. Manchester's 'blitz' was concentrated in the two nights of 22 and 23 December 1940.

In Manchester, Salford and the surrounding area the bombs started 1,300 fires on those two December nights in 1940. Firemen had to fight for two days and three nights to bring them under control. The work was prolonged by a strong north-east wind which arose early on Christmas Eve, fanned the embers, and drove the fires again through the warehouses and offices. It was not until Christmas

171

Day that the fires started by the incendiary bombs were at last under control. One contemporary journalist described the ordeal of the firefighters:

> Fatigued almost beyond endurance by their efforts, sodden and frozen by the cascades of water streaming from doomed buildings, or from the jets trained on them by their colleagues, to enable them to keep at close grips with the flames which scorched them, they worked on. ('Our Blitz', *Daily Despatch and Evening Chronicle,* Manchester)

The other services worked at full stretch too: civil defence, ARP, hospitals and mobile canteens to name but a few.

The destruction was enormous. Within a mile radius of Albert Square, over 31 acres (12 ha) were reduced to ruins. Among famous buildings destroyed were the Free Trade Hall, the Royal Exchange and Cross Street Chapel, all subsequently rebuilt. Among the irreparable damage was the destruction of the scientific collection belonging to the Manchester Literary and Philosophical Society in George Street, including Dalton's apparatus for formulating his Atomic Theory. Large numbers of schools were destroyed, including the newly finished High School for Girls. Many churches, too, were extensively damaged. One bomb struck the north-east corner of Manchester Cathedral (formerly the Collegiate Church). The Dean, Dr Garfield Williams, who was watching at the time, described its effect:

> The blast had lifted the whole lead roof of the Cathedral up and then dropped it back, miraculously, in place. Every window and door had gone; chairs, ornaments, carpets, furnishings, had been just swept up into the air and dropped in heaps anywhere. The High Altar was just a heap of rubbish ten feet high.

Apart from the holocaust of public and commercial buildings, 30,000 homes were damaged or destroyed in Manchester and a further 8,000 in Salford. In Manchester, over 5,000 homeless people sought temporary accommodation in the 28 rest centres. Some had had narrow escapes. Two people in Salford were in bed when a bomb dropped in the street outside, and they 'slithered down through collapsing bricks and slates, still on the mattress which came to rest in the crater, with its astonished "passengers" practically unhurt'. In the suburbs some families were saved by spending the nights of the raids in their Anderson shelters.

Christmas was spent clearing up the rubble. Even for those houses that had escaped without even shattered windows, there was the problem of the grey dust which filled the atmosphere for days after the attack. Festivities were muted. Only Christmas Day was taken as a holiday, and even Father Christmas seemed more concerned with war causes, like collecting salvage, than with his traditional duties. No bells were rung on Christmas morning, but large congregations were noted in the churches. There were football matches in the afternoon, but crowds were small. Only 1,500 watched Manchester United beat Stockport County 3-1, at Edgeley Park. United's ground had been rendered temporarily unusable by the bombing. In the evening dance-halls opened by special permission of the magistrates.

For Manchester and Salford, 1940 was the worst Christmas of the war. Enemy bombardment had done enormous damage, as the King and Queen witnessed when they visited the scene in February 1941. A total of 560 people had been killed and 632 seriously injured in the two cities. Yet morale was upheld in spite of the ordeal and strengthened by the rapid recovery. Although Exchange Station had been destroyed and one whole railway viaduct had collapsed, transport was soon back to normal. Trafford Park, the main industrial centre, had got off remarkably lightly. The destruction gave a new purpose to the peace which eventually followed, and the opportunity which seemed to many to be heaven-sent, of replacing some of the worst legacies of the nineteenth century.

Liverpool suffered even more than Manchester from aerial bombardment, and the end of the war left the city with an enormous housing problem. One solution was to continue the policy of large housing estates on the fringe of the city, such as the pre-war developments at Speke and Norris Green. A shortage of available land made the Liverpool Corporation look further afield. Sites were needed for both industrial and housing purposes, and the new-town movement of the inter-war years was a strong influence on the planners.

With all this in mind, the war-time ordnance factory at Kirkby, to the east of Liverpool and surrounded by open fields, seemed an attractive site for new corporation housing. Although outside the city boundaries, the heart of the projected town was only seven miles from Pier Head. Formerly prime agricultural land, the site was purchased by Liverpool Corporation from the Earl of Sefton in 1947.

173

Liverpool originally intended a satellite 'community unit' on the lines of pre-war developments, but it proved impossible to extend the city boundaries so far and still fulfil green belt requirements between Kirkby and Liverpool. Intended as an overspill estate, Kirkby gradually emerged as a new town. It did not, however, enjoy the privileged treatment of most post-war new towns. Its main purpose had been to solve Liverpool's housing shortage, and to do this it had to grow at incredible speed. Work started in 1952 and by 1959 over 10,000 dwellings had been built. The population came in as fast as the houses and flats went up: from 3,210 in 1951 Kirkby had grown to 52,139 by 1961. Not even the mushroom towns of the nineteenth century could equal this growth.

Most of the arrivals came from Liverpool, particularly from the bombed areas near the docks and from slum housing around the university. The move was traumatic for many of the families concerned. They came from overcrowded tenements in worn-out nineteenth-century areas of the city centre, to find themselves in the middle of the Lancashire countryside in entirely different circumstances. The houses and flats were all brand new, but all the shops, pubs, clubs and other facilities, which in Liverpool had been only just round the corner, were now a seven-mile tram or bus journey away. The survey of newcomers' attitudes to Kirkby by K.G. Pickett and D.K. Boulton in 1961 showed that some of the families had never lived in flats before; many were separated from old friends and relatives; and all were affected by higher rents — in spite of corporation subsidies — and the lack of facilities. Priority had been given to housing because of necessity and, except for schools, most other buildings were left until later. After the wealth of social life available in the city, Kirkby seemed like a desert to the newcomers. Its lifeline was the bus service to Pier Head. Over half the new townsfolk were Roman Catholics. Fortunately for Kirkby, their church acted swiftly and sponsored a great variety of activities. As J.B. Mays, the sociologist, wrote in *New Society* in 1963: 'Had the Catholic Church not been ready for the waves of new arrivals who descended upon Kirkby from its inception in 1952 to the virtual completion in the early 1960s, social life might well have broken down entirely'.

Kirkby's great asset was the clean and healthy environment it could provide for the young, who made up the majority of the population. The housing was well laid out in community areas with all 'mod cons'. The council, which owned over 90% of the dwellings, took a justifiable pride in the fact that in 1971 Kirkby had the highest proportion of households with exclusive use of hot water supply, fixed bath and inside flush toilet of any area in Lancashire. In this respect the dream of generations of health officers, planners and philanthropists had come true.

Yet if Kirkby represented the fulfilment of a dream, it also presented problems of a disturbing kind. The town was dominated from the outset by youth. Even in 1971, half the population was below 22 years of age. They had benefited from a far healthier upbringing than many of their parents had known, and from the great efforts of the schools and youth organizations. They had suffered, however, from the dislocation of family backgrounds, from the initial lack of facilities, from the town's class and age imbalance, and from the unsettling vision of better planned and in some ways more attractive new towns at Skelmersdale and Runcorn.

The *Z Cars* image of the late 1950s was no doubt unfair and locally much resented, but even when the town had settled down a number of serious headaches remained. The fine new housing, as in other urban areas, brought unexpected difficulties. Tower blocks caused social and psychological problems and were found to be very unsuitable for young families. In Kirkby the medium-rise, three-storey flats were more common and bore the main brunt of criticism. Many families were disappointed to receive such accommodation when they had expected, by moving to Kirkby, to obtain a house. There were complaints that the flats were too small, too noisy and too expensive. Problem families were said to have a demoralizing effect on a whole block of flats. The result was a vicious circle of non-payment of rents, vandalism and a high turnover of tenants. Rent arrears and a huge backlog of repairs weighed increasingly on a local authority which, by the mid-1970s was facing Whitehall's demands for cutbacks in local government expenditure.

Employment problems added to Kirkby's troubles in the 1970s. In 1972-5 the town's unemployment rate was three times the national average. The effect on a town so full of young people and with a relatively immobile labour force caused more than local concern. The town received the first Job Centre in the country, a variety of training programmes and work schemes and a good deal of government aid.

Many of Kirkby's difficulties were national ones writ large.

Great efforts were made by the town's leaders, teachers and social workers, often with insufficient recognition. The town's facilities continued to expand. By 1975 the headmaster of Eton could describe one Kirkby school as in certain ways better equipped than his own. The town's sporting facilities became the envy of the north-west: the Athletic Stadium could boast that John Conteh, one-time world light heavy-weight champion who came from the area, had first trained there.

As for the county in general, its main changes in social life since 1945 can only be summarized here. In terms of employment, the region saw the rapid run-down of the cotton industry after 1951. The decline might have been even faster if it had not been for some restrictions on imports from the Commonwealth. Bolton, for example, which still had 103 cotton mills in 1957, had only 34 by 1966 and merely 8 by 1979. Other towns showed a similar pattern. The Cotton Industry Act of 1959 led to the rapid dismantling of machinery and conversion of premises, in some cases to the production of man-made fibres.

One of the major sources of new employment was the car industry. This played a particularly important role in the revival of Merseyside, with a Ford plant at Halewood, Standard-Triumph at Speke, and Vauxhall Motors across the river at Ellesmere Port. A big expansion also took place in Leyland Motors at Leyland, whose buses and trucks established a world-wide reputation. Meanwhile the growth of electrical engineering and the aircraft industries provided many new jobs in the Preston area. In the north, the Barrow shipyards had turned from building liners to oil and gas tankers, and from conventional to nuclear submarines. Resorts like Blackpool and Morecambe faced the problem of the popularity of holidays abroad. Farming also changed considerably, with barley replacing oats and wheat as the major crop in parts of south Lancashire. Market gardening and pig-farms became more extensive, while further north many dairy farms survived, supplemented by egg and poultry production.

In demographic terms, the north-west ceased to lose as many people by migration as in the 1920s, although some urban areas acquired a 'ghost-town' appearance as a result of population movement and redevelopment. West Indian and Asian immigration added new ingredients to the already cosmopolitan character of many towns. Traditional clogs and shawls disappeared and in some parts were replaced by sandals and saris.

Taking stock at the end of the 1970s it was clear that much of the adaptation of the north-west to new patterns of life had been successful. The face of the county had been transformed in the generation since the Second World War by new towns and suburbs and by the rebuilding of town centres with office blocks and market areas. Most noticeable perhaps was the network of motorways — 280 miles (450 km) by 1 January 1980 — strung across the landscape, linking towns and giving rapid access to the seaside and the hills. Meanwhile the electrification of the main rail links had brought Lancashire within two and a half hours of London. At Manchester (Ringway) and Liverpool (Speke) the region could boast two international airports. Liverpool was still the second largest port in the UK in terms of tonnage handled and Manchester the sixth. The nuclear power station at Heysham, started in 1970, is expected to provide one third of the region's needs by 1981.

In terms of population, wages and employment, however, Lancashire's position by comparison with the rest of the United Kingdom was less favourable in the 1970s than it had been a hundred years before. In 1971 the population of the ancient county stood at 5,118,423 or 9% of the UK total, compared to 11% in 1901. After enjoying wage levels well above the national average in the eighteenth and nineteenth centuries, the average Lancastrian had to accept a less favourable position in the twentieth. Although certain costs such as housing were lower in the north-west than in the country as a whole, money wages stood below the national average. It is notable that the number of women in employment in the north-west remained at its traditionally high level. Unemployment was also high; it stood at 8% in the north-west (12% in Liverpool) in November 1977, compared with the national figure of 6%. Whereas the north-west had accounted for 13% of the national unemployment in 1968, it accounted for 15% by 1978. The rate of capital formation had meanwhile declined.

There were other problems too. As the country's most highly urbanized region, the north-west still had a particularly large legacy of obsolescent buildings — and also, as became clear, of outworn sewers — along with other unwanted bequests of the Industrial Revolution, such as air and river pollution and derelict land. The physical environment had been improved by the Clean Air Acts and by the change from king coal to gas, electricity and oil. Government money had been made available for reclamation of land and for

177

the cleaning of public buildings and churches. Conservation came to be considered as relevant to Lancashire, and in important cases, like Arkwright House, Preston, the bulldozer, delayed by the slowness of redevelopment, was stayed altogether. Local history and archaeological societies became popular, while museums, record offices and universities (including the Universities of Lancaster and Salford, chartered in 1964 and 1967 respectively) helped provide the leadership and scholarship necessary for the intelligent preservation of the region's heritage.

In social terms the quality of life remained as rich as ever. Music and the theatre participated in the national revival, while sport, both amateur and professional, enjoyed an enthusiastic and often boisterous following. In spite of the increased mobility of the population and urban redevelopment, the traditional gregarious spirit, as measured in the number of pubs, clubs and churches, and sentimentalized for the whole nation by the Granada TV series *Coronation Street* (launched in 1960), continued as a reality all over Lancashire. The high circulation of local newspapers (not to mention the success of the *Guardian* as a national newspaper from 1960) showed the close identification of many people with both the local and regional community. Civic pride and confidence in the future, so characteristic of Victorian Lancashire, lived on, in spite of modern scepticism. In Liverpool those two great Victorian dreams, a Roman Catholic and an Anglican cathedral, were at last fulfilled — the former in 1967 and the latter in 1978. The Industrial Revolution had left many problems, but it had fostered a local pride, a distinctive character and sense of humour which the twentieth century could not destroy.

> Down our street
> There are married men and women there
> Dancing mad in the midnight air
> Lots of jawbones missing, where?
> Down our street.

Mike Harding © 1976
Reproduced by permission of EMI
Publishing Ltd from *Napoleon's Retreat from Wigan*
by Mike Harding

FURTHER READING

1 Origins

Farrer, W., and Brownhill, J., ed., *Victoria County History of Lancashire*, 8 vols., 1906-14

Bagley, J.J., *Lancashire*, Batsford, 1972

Bagley, J.J., *A History of Lancashire*, Darwen Finlayson, 1970

Bagley, J.J., *Lancashire Diaries*, Phillimore, 1975

Marshall, J.D., *Lancashire,* David and Charles, 1974

Freeman, T.W., Rodgers, H.B., Kinvig, R.H., *Lancashire, Cheshire and the Isle of Man*, Nelson, 1966

Corry, J., *The Works of Tim Bobbin in Prose and Verse*, Rochdale, 1819

Bobbin, T., *Human Passions Delineated,* Rochdale, 1773 reprinted E.J. Morten, 1972

King, A., *Early Pennine Settlement*, Dalesman, 1970

2 The Roman Occupation

Watkin, W.T., *Roman Lancashire*, Liverpool, 1883, reprinted, E.P. Publishing 1969

Shotter, D.C.A., *Romans in Lancashire,* Dalesman, 1973

Garlick, T., *Romans in the Lake Counties,* Dalesman, 1972

Jones, G.D.B., ed., *Roman Manchester,* Sherratt, 1974

Edwards, B.J.N., *Ribchester,* National Trust, 1972

For news of current digs and the latest finds, consult *Contrebis* (the Bulletin of the Lancaster Archaeological Society) and the *Ribble Archaeological Society Bulletin*

3 Saxons and Vikings

Ekwall, E., *The Place-Names of Lancashire*, 1922, reprinted, E.P. Publishing 1972

Mills, D., *Place-Names of Lancashire,* Batsford 1976

Wainwright, F.T., 'The Anglian Settlement of Lancashire', *Transactions of the Historic Society of Lancashire and Cheshire,* vol. 93, 1941

Wainwright, F.T., 'The Scandinavians in Lancashire', *Transactions of the Lancashire and Cheshire Antiquarian Society,* vol. 58, 1945-6

Garmonsway, G.N., ed., *The Anglo Saxon Chronicle,* Everyman, 1972

Sterling, J., *Dark Age and Norman Lancashire,* Dalesman, 1974

4 Mediaeval Lancashire

Victoria County History, Vols. I and II.

Darby, H.C., and Maxwell, I.S., ed., *The Domesday Geography of Northern England,* Cambridge University Press, 1962

Cunliffe Shaw, R., *The Royal Forest of Lancaster,* privately printed, Preston, 1956

Tait, J., *Mediaeval Manchester and the Beginnings of Lancashire,* 1904, reprint E.J. Morten, 1972

Knowles, D., *The Monastic Orders in England,* Cambridge University Press, 1949

Sharpe France, R., 'The Customs of the Manor of Cockerham', *Trans. Lancs. Chesh. Antiquarian Society,* vol. 64, 1954

Sharpe France, R., 'The Stanley Account Roll, 1460', *Trans. Historic Soc. Lancs. Chesh.,* vol. 113, 1961

Ashmore, O., 'Whalley Abbey Bursar's Account for 1520', *Trans. Historic Soc. Lancs. Chesh.,* Vol. 114, 1962

Dickinson, J.C., *Furness Abbey,* HMSO, 1966

Beamont, W., ed., *Warrington in 1465,* Chetham Society, XVII, Manchester, 1849

Tomkeieff, O.G., *Life in Norman England,* Batsford, 1966

Bagley, J.J., *Life in Medieval England,* Batsford, 1960

5 Tudor and early Stuart Times

Haigh, C., *The Last Days of the Lancashire Monasteries,* Chetham Society, Manchester, 1969

Haigh, C., *Reformation and Resistance in Tudor Lancashire,* Cambridge University Press, 1975

Tupling, G.H., *An Economic History of Rossendale,* Chetham

Society, Manchester, 1927

Wadsworth, A.P., and de L. Mann, J., *The Cotton Trade and Industrial Lancashire*, Manchester University, 1931

Lowe, N., *The Lancashire Textile Industry in the Sixteenth Century*, Chetham Society, Manchester, 1972

Thomson, W.H., *History of·Manchester to 1852*, Sherratt, 1967

Richardson, R.C., *Puritanism in North-West England*, Manchester University, 1972

Leatherbarrow, J.S., *The Lancashire Elizabethan Recusants*, Chetham Society, Manchester, 1947

Thomas, K., *Religion and the Decline of Magic*, Weidenfeld and Nicolson, 1971

Peel, E., and Southern, P., *The Trials of the Lancashire Witches*, David and Charles, 1969

Sterling, J., *Elizabethan and Jacobean Lancashire*, Dalesman, 1973

Williams, P., *Life in Tudor England*, Batsford, 1964

Dodd, A.H., *Life in Elizabethan England*, Batsford, 1961

6 From the Civil War to The Forty-Five

Sharpe France, R., 'A History of the Plague in Lancashire', *Trans. Historic Soc. Lancs. Chesh.*, vol. 90, 1938

Tupling, G.H., 'The Causes of the Civil War in Lancashire', *Trans. Lancs. Chesh. Antiquarian Society*, vol. 65, 1955

Broxap, E., *The Great Civil War in Lancashire*, Manchester, 1910

Dore, R.N., *The Great Civil War in the Manchester Area*, BBC Radio Manchester, 1973

Sterling, J., *The Civil War in Lancashire*, Dalesman, 1973

Parkinson, R., ed., *The Life of Adam Martindale*, Chetham Society IV, 1844

Halley, R., *Lancashire, its Puritanism and Nonconformity*, 2 vols. 1869

Parkinson, R., ed., *The Autobiography of Henry Newcome*, Chetham Society, 2 vols., 1852

Tyrer, F., *The Great Diurnall of Nicholas Blundell*, 3 vols., Record Society of Lancashire and Cheshire, 1968, 1970, 1972

Sterling, J., *The Jacobite Rebellions in Lancashire*, Dalesman, 1973

Marshall, J.D., ed., *The Autobiography of William Stout of Lancaster*, Manchester University, 1967

Ashley, M., *Life in Stuart England*, Batsford, 1964

7 The Industrial Revolution

Hyde, F.E., *Liverpool and the Mersey: An Economic History of the Port 1700-1970,* David and Charles, 1971

Moss, W., *The Liverpool Guide,* 1796, reprint City of Liverpool, 1974

Moss, W., *Liverpool and Slavery,* 1884, reprint Frank Graham, 1969

Martin, B., and Spurrell, M., ed., *The Journal of a Slave Trader,* Epworth, 1962

Hadfield, C., and Biddle, G., *The Canals of North West England,* 2 vols. David and Charles, 1970

French, G.J., *Life and Times of Samuel Crompton,* 1859, reprinted Adams and Dart, 1970

Smelser, N., *Social Change in the Industrial Revolution,* Routledge, 1959

Collier, F., *The Family Economy of the Working Classes in the Cotton Industry, 1784-1833,* Chetham Society, Manchester, 1965

Holt, J., *General View of the Agriculture of the County of Lancaster,* 1795, reprint David and Charles, 1969

Williams, E.N., *Life in Georgian England,* Batsford, 1962

8 The Age of Steam

Baines, E., *History of the Cotton Manufacture in Great Britain,* 1935, reprint Frank Cass, 1966

Chapple, J.A.V., and Pollard, A., ed., *The Letters of Mrs Gaskell,* Manchester University, 1966

Aspin, C., *Lancashire, the First Industrial Society,* Helmshore Local History Society, 1969

Anderson, M., *Family Structure in Nineteenth Century Lancashire,* Cambridge University Press, 1971

Clapp, B.W., *John Owens, Manchester Merchant,* Manchester University, 1965

Briggs, A., *Victorian Cities,* Odhams, 1963, Pelican, 1968

Perkin, H., *The Age of the Railway,* Panther, 1970

Carlson, R.E., *The Liverpool and Manchester Project, 1821-31,* David and Charles, 1969

Brown, W.E., *Robert Heywood of Bolton,* S.R., 1970

Bythell, D., *The Handloom Weavers,* Cambridge University Press, 1969

Challinor, R., *The Lancashire and Cheshire Miners,* Frank Graham, 1972

Briggs, A., ed., *Chartist Studies,* Macmillan, 1959

Waugh, E., *Lancashire Sketches,* John Heywood, 1869

Ellison, M., *Support for Secession: Lancashire and the American Civil War,* Chicago University, 1972

9 Late Victorian and Edwardian Hey-day

Pevsner, N., *The Buildings of England: Lancashire,* 2 vols., Penguin, 1969

Ashmore, O., *Industrial Archaeology of Lancashire,* David and Charles, 1969

Roberts, R., *The Classic Slum,* Manchester University, 1971, Pelican, 1973

Caminada, J., *Twenty-Five Years of Detective Life,* 2 vols., Manchester, 1895 and 1901

Bell, S.P., ed., *Victorian Lancashire,* David and Charles, 1974

Charlton, H.B., *Portrait of a University, 1851-1951,* Manchester, 1951

Tylecote, M., *The Education of Women at Manchester University 1833-1933,* Manchester, 1941

Dobbs, B., *Edwardians at Play,* Pelham, 1973

Nowell-Smith, S., ed., *Edwardian England,* Oxford University Press, 1964

Flintoff, T.R., *Preston Guild Merchant,* Kraymar, Preston, 1972

Mould, G., *Manchester Memories,* Terence Dalton, 1972

Clarke, P.F., *Lancashire and the New Liberalism,* Cambridge University Press, 1971

Williams, Bill, *The Making of Manchester Jewry, 1740-1875,* Manchester University Press, 1976

Eyre, K., *Seven Golden Miles,* Weaver and Youles, 1961

Ledbrooke, A.W., *Lancashire County Cricket, 1864-1953,* 1954

Churchill, R.S., *Lord Derby, 'King of Lancashire',* Heinemann, 1959

Fletcher, T.W., 'Lancashire livestock farming during the Great Depression', *Agricultural History Review,* IX, 1961

Cecil, R., *Life in Edwardian England,* Batsford, 1969

10 The Twentieth Century

Bowker, B., *Lancashire under the Hammer,* Hogarth, 1928

Sandberg, L.G., *Lancashire in Decline,* Ohio, 1974

Whittington-Egan, R., *Liverpool Soundings,* Gallery, 1969

'Our Blitz', *Daily Despatch and Evening Chronicle*, Manchester Public Libraries

Pickett, K.G., and Boulton, D.K., *Migration and Social Adjustment,* Liverpool University, 1974

Seabrook, J., *City Close-Up,* Allen Lane, 1971

Turner, G., *The Leyland Papers,* Eyre and Spottiswood, 1971

Channon, H., *Portrait of Liverpool,* Robert Hale, 1970

Kennedy, M., *Portrait of Manchester,* Robert Hale, 1970

Smith, D.M., *The North West,* David and Charles, 1969

Strategic Plan for the North West: SPNW Joint Planning Team Report 1973, H.M.S.O., 1974

INDEX

The numerals in **bold type** refer to the illustration numbers

185